LITTLE WONDER

LITTLE WONDER

*or, The Reader's Digest
and how it grew*

by John Bainbridge

051

REYNAL & HITCHCOCK, NEW YORK

Printed in the U. S. A. ◆◆◆ı   by The Cornwall Press, Inc.

To D. H. B.

ACKNOWLEDGMENT

A considerable portion of this book first appeared in *The New Yorker,* to which the author makes grateful acknowledgment.

CONTENTS

1. WALLY   1

2. BIRTH OF AN ARISTOCRAT   26

3. PLANT YOU NOW, DIG YOU LATER   52

4. CHAPPAQUA, U.S.A.   76

5. ELEVEN MILLION COPIES,
   INCLUDING THE SCANDINAVIAN   112

6. DR. WALLACE'S MAGIC FORMULA   133

LITTLE WONDER

1

WALLY

AS a publishing phenomenon, *The Reader's Digest* compares favorably with the Holy Bible. Except for the Scriptures, nothing ever published has been circulated more widely than the *Digest*. Like the Bible, the *Digest* is printed in many tongues and distributed on all continents. The Bible is currently available in one thousand and sixty-eight languages and dialects, and the *Digest* is printed only in American, British, Canadian, Spanish, Portuguese, Swedish, Arabic, Chinese, Finnish, Danish, Braille, and Talking-Record editions, but it must be remembered that the Bible had a head start. The *Digest* is catching up rapidly and before long it will be offered in more languages and possibly a few dialects. Even with its present limitations, it is doing all right. In 1944, the American Bible Society and the British and

Foreign Bible Society, the two largest organizations devoted to circulating Holy Writ, together distributed nineteen million volumes of Scripture. During the same period, the *Digest* was bought by more than eleven million people every month. That represents a modest increase of only a million copies over the year before, but nobody on the *Digest* doubts that a great day is coming.

In spreading their gospels, both Christian missionaries and *Digest* representatives occasionally encounter a little sales resistance from certain of the heathen. Pagans here and there show reluctance to accept the Bible or the *Digest* as hallowed literature. The Christian and *Digest* missionaries meet this situation with serenity. "No criticism of the Bible has ever hurt it very much and it has been criticized plenty," a *Digest* field worker has said, "and no criticism has ever hurt *The Reader's Digest* very much and it has been criticized plenty." There is a good deal of truth in what the man says, for the *Digest*, like the Bible, has a way of inspiring devotion that sometimes borders on fanaticism. "I can but say thank God for the *Digest!*" a man from Chicago exclaimed in one of the thousands of testimonials received

every year at *Digest* headquarters. Actors have
said the *Digest* gives them faith and cures nerv-
ousness and that they therefore read it while waiting for their cues. Doctors have said they read it
while delivering babies, farmers while milking,
pilots while flying, businessmen while shaving and
bathing, old women while churning, and young
women while nursing their infants. Whenever she
feels a spell of depression coming on, a lady in
Salt Lake City has testified, she reaches for her
Digest. "This tonic," she has written, "never
fails to chase away the blues." Her findings have
been corroborated by a prominent medical authority. Dr. Herman N. Bundesen, president of the
Chicago Board of Health, has said that eight or
ten times a month he prescribes an issue of the
Digest to a patient suffering from worry, fear, or
hypochondria. Additional proof of the *Digest's*
hidden and often unsuspected powers was discovered after a bad bus accident in San Francisco.
Rescue workers, pulling the wreckage apart, found
a man whose nose, legs, and ribs had been shat-
tered. He was reading his *Digest* and seemed to be
suffering no pain. The testimonial that has pleased
the *Digest* people most (they have printed it on

their back cover twice) was offered during the war by a person identified as "a reader who came out with General MacArthur from the Philippines." It said, "In the hospital on Bataan there were just two battered copies of *The Reader's Digest,* and the fellows ate them up. I took one with me when we got onto the sub with the MacArthur party. In those ten days on the sub we took turns reading and rereading the magazine—General MacArthur and all of us. I've still got that copy in my locker. Never will part with it." It is a relic worth preserving, since Commander Bulkeley and a number of other reliable men swear that they took General MacArthur from the Philippines to Australia in a PT boat and a Flying Fortress. The General's mysterious appearance in a submarine to read a few *Digest* articles ranks as one of the minor miracles of our times.

To be head of as potent an enterprise as *The Reader's Digest* would be enough to bewitch an average editor into believing himself something of a messiah. DeWitt Wallace, the fifty-six-year-old editor of *The Reader's Digest,* is not average. If he has any messianic notions about himself, he has shown few of the familiar symptoms. Wallace is the most successful editor in history because he knows probably better than any other man alive what people want to read. His talent for divining what sociologists call the mass mind is enjoyed, to a lesser degree, by such eminent editors as Henry Luce, Bernarr Macfadden, and William Randolph Hearst, all of whom have indicated that the possession of the editorial gift can give a man ambitious ideas about himself. At one time or another, Hearst, Luce, and Macfadden have all fallen under the spell of thinking that because they feed reading matter to millions they are also cut out to lead them, possibly as President of the United States. Wallace, being endowed so much more richly than any of his colleagues, as the circulation figures show, might well be expected to share some of their grandiose ideas. This is not the case. He has no delusions of grandeur. He has, if anything, delusions of smallness. To Wallace, most things, including himself, seem smaller than they actually are.

Although Wallace operates globally, he thinks locally. He calls the *Digest* headquarters, a million-dollar building on the outskirts of Chappaqua, a small suburb of New York City, "the shop" and his employees, numbering twenty-five hundred at the peak of the year, "the folks who work with us." He encourages his impressively large staff of fifty-two editors, whom he refers to as "the bunch of boys who get out the magazine," to call him by his nickname, Wally. They do. Lest the folks who worked with him would think he was putting on executive airs, he refused for years to have a secretary. He has one now, but anybody who wants to talk with the editor of the *Digest* has only to call Chappaqua 400 and ask for him; phone calls for Wallace are put through to him direct. Talking with people both in his organization and out of it, Wallace seems as persistent as Dr. Gallup in his quest for other people's opinions. He is diffident about his own. Editors of other magazines have found that no matter what aspect of the publishing business they try to discuss with him, he usually hedges by saying, "Well, what do you think? You know more about these things than I do." This habit, according to one venerable editor, is more disconcerting than flattering. "There," he has said, "sits Wallace, the greatest editor the world has ever seen, asking me what *I* think. It's as crazy as Einstein asking a schoolboy how to handle fractions." Wallace once sent a *Digest* editor around the country to ask a number of prominent citizens to give their conception of a significant magazine article, and he also once made a rather ingenuous effort to engage a well-known author to hang around other important magazine editors to find out what was on their minds and relay it to him. That many of his colleagues are equally curious to know what is on his mind has apparently never occurred to Wallace. He just lacks the power to see himself as big as others see him.

From South Dakota to Saudi Arabia, large segments of the human race are familiar with the *Digest's* format, but few people are familiar with Wallace's. This is mainly because Wallace doesn't like to have his picture taken. Several years ago, when *Fortune* was preparing an article about the *Digest,* Wallace forbade its photographers to come nearer to him than the threshold of his office. "I'm not important," he kept saying. In the one authorized photograph of Wallace now in existence, the editor of the *Digest,* wearing a constrained smile, looks as theatrical and smooth as Herbert Marshall. Actually, he looks as plain and unpretentious as his magazine. He is tall, sturdy, and slightly stooped. He is generally considered good-looking, but not in an imposing or bizarre way. His features are regular and his jaw is firm; he has receding, iron-gray hair, blue eyes of an indeterminate shade, and deep lines running from his nose to his mouth. For trips to the city he dresses with taste and, except for gay haberdashery, conservatively. In the country he goes in for tweeds in winter and rayon slack suits and two-toned sports shoes in summer. Like Luce, Wallace speaks haltingly and tends to give his auditors the uneasy feeling that he never quite says all he might, but he has little of Luce's austerity. "Wally isn't exactly a hail-fellow," a writer who has worked for both Luce and Wallace has said, "but when you meet him on the street you feel like inviting him into a bar for a drink and a chat. With Luce, you say how do you do and keep moving." Wallace, more a sociable than a convivial drinker, frequently asks what his companion is having and then orders the same. His magazine has for years carried on a spirited anti-cigarette crusade, but he is a backslider who gets away with a couple of packs a day.

Aside from its position on smokes, the *Digest* is a faithful image of its editor. The truism that magazines, like children, reflect the men who beget and rear them has never been more satisfyingly illustrated than by the *Digest*. There is all the more reason for the resemblance in this case, because Wallace not only conceived the magazine but, with his wife, also founded the enterprise, has always edited it, and owns it outright. The *Digest* is Wallace's baby, and it reflects nearly everything about its father, from his capsulated social and economic opinions down to his taste in humor. Every once in a while the *Digest* comes out with a remarkably risqué joke. So does Wallace. "Wally likes jokes," a *Digest* editor has explained. "And they don't have to be Methodist jokes, either." Wallace is not a Methodist but a Presbyterian, the son of a rugged Doctor of Divinity. Wallace, who is rebellious to the point of not being a churchgoing man, nevertheless believes in the Golden Rule, in helping the deserving poor, and in promoting good works. He is full of good intentions. "He is a man," one of his literary friends once remarked, "of complete and bewildered good will," an appraisal that could describe, with equal clarity and charity, his journalistic offspring. Most people who talk to Wallace or read his magazine get the impression that this is not only the best of all possible worlds but also an astonishingly small one. Wallace's approach to the employment problem in the postwar world, for example, is characteristically goodhearted and minuscule. He gave away $25,000 in prizes to *Digest* readers who contributed ideas for small businesses in which returning service men might set themselves up. Among the prize-winners were suggestions that veterans could earn a living by polishing floors, making dolls, selling second-hand baby furniture, and, if they had enough capital to buy a jeep, becoming delivery boys. The plan, benevolent though possibly not entirely adequate, had a surface simplicity that appealed to Wallace, whose economic views are somewhat compressed. One of the most memorable industrial articles the *Digest* has ever printed was a passionate attack on men who repair watches.

Wallace's small-scale view of life is a priceless asset. It has made him a multi-millionaire and gained him recognition as a genius. "He's a genius, all right, and a greater genius than Hearst," an old and worldly friend of his once said. "He has a more perfect understanding of the herd mind. Wallace looks at the universe constantly through the wrong end of the telescope, and so does the herd. He sees everything neat and tidy, and so do they. He knows what they want, and he lets them have it." How Wallace knows what the mass of humanity wants is a mystery, like Creation. The way his mind works baffles amateur analysts, among them several *Digest* editors who have worked in close contact with him for from ten to twenty years. About all they have been able to conclude is that he is intuitive rather than intellectual, that his opinions are subject to change without notice, and that ideas seem to have to run a kind of obstacle race before they can penetrate his mind. At a week-end party in Connecticut a while ago, a *Digest* editor wandered in, had a short drink, and offered a condensed analysis of Wallace which may be as sound as any. "Wally is like a bat," the roving editor said. "Science has never discovered how a bat is able to find its way in the dark, and nobody knows how Wally is able to find his. He simply has a batlike instinct for finding his way journalistically. He's flying blind, but he's a genius just the same.''

The custom of calling Wallace a genius is widespread, but there are those among his acquaintances who assert that the term is more useful than accurate. They argue that the difference between genuine genius and Wallace's conspicuous talent is like the difference between fifteen-year-old genuine Scotch whiskey and domestic concoctions known as ''Scotch-type'' whiskey; the latter has the general appearance and the primary effect of the real article but contains a certain number of foreign ingredients, such as prune juice. These hairsplitters contend that Wallace is not a genuine genius but merely an authentic genius-type, or what might be called a genuine mock genius. As some of his followers, both friendly and unfriendly, have discovered, however, it is handy to describe him merely as a genius, because the term, in its popular sense, now simply connotes exceptional talent accompanied by exceptional eccentricity. Like most editors, Wallace has many idiosyncrasies, and since he is at the head of his profession, he may have, and indeed may be entitled to, a few more than the usual complement.

As every writer knows, editors are as unpredictable as the weather. However, after dealing with any one of them over a long period, a writer usually feels capable of making some general forecasts about his man. Writers who have dealt with Wallace for years say they have developed as much confidence in their ability to guess his reactions as a weather man who can't tell whether tomorrow will be winter or summer. Their recollections of conferences with Wallace about original articles, of which the *Digest,* supposedly a publication devoted to printing condensations of pieces that have already appeared elsewhere, prints a surprisingly large number, follow a pattern. The routine begins when the writer is invited to Chappaqua for lunch. A senior editor of the *Digest* shepherds him up from town on the train, and the two men talk over the writer's ideas en route. "That's a natural," or "Wally will go for that one," the editor is apt to say confidently about two or three of the ideas, and the author accordingly puts these first on his agenda. Arriving in Chappaqua, he and the editor are joined by

Wallace and possibly a couple of other *Digest* editors, and if it is summertime, the party may drive to a cozy near-by tearoom, which has tables on the lawn and serves a pleasant sixty-five-cent blue plate. After a single sherry and a round of non-Methodist jokes, the author gets a chance to discuss his ideas.

He starts, of course, with the ones he has been assured Wallace will go for. Wallace almost never shows any interest in these. By the time lunch is finished, the author has exhausted both his preferred and common ideas and Wallace has begun to drum nervously on the table. "That's not quite what I had in mind," Wallace is likely to say when an idea is advanced, and then turn to his subordinate editors and ask, "What do you think?" "Not quite what I had in mind, either, Wally," they are apt to say, almost, and sometimes actually, at once. "I want something absolutely original," Wallace may continue. "I'll pay fifteen thousand dollars for a great article." Instead of inspiring a writer, the mention of this sum is likely to depress him. He thinks of all the things he could do with fifteen thousand dollars and at the same time realizes that he has a miserably slim chance of doing them, for if his best idea isn't worth a dime, how is he going to get one worth fifteen grand? The author's world suddenly looks black. Flies are stinging him under the table, worms from the trees overhead are dropping softly onto his plate, and, limp and morose, he falls into a tortured reverie. Sometimes, on such occasions, Wallace breaks in with a question like "Tell me, what's new in plastics?" If the writer happens to know of a recent development in that field, he may arouse Wallace's interest and wind up with an assignment to write an article on the topic. If no acceptable ideas are forthcoming, Wallace may ask, "Were you planning to catch the two-forty-three back to town? That's a good train."

Some writers, especially those who might be classed as minor celebrities, fare much better with Wallace, for a while. Despite his own towering position as a journalist, Wallace is still easily awed by prosperous professional writers, and has a habit of taking a sudden, though short-lived, fancy to one of them. One of his great favorites is Louis Bromfield, who has contributed a number of absolutely original articles to the *Digest*. "Wallace buys articles the way an art collector buys

pictures," a jilted Wallace favorite once said.
"He doesn't buy an article by Bromfield, he buys
a Bromfield." Unquestionably the most famous
Bromfield that Wallace has acquired was published in August, 1943, under the title "We Aren't
Going to Have Enough to Eat." This piece, which
predicted a perilous food shortage, attracted international attention and was reprinted by the Ger-
man Propaganda Ministry. Other Bromfields have
had a somewhat narrower appeal; his *Digest*
essay on the artificial insemination of cows, for
example, was considered a museum piece by few
connoisseurs outside the Grange. While he is col-
lecting an author, Wallace behaves like a patron of
the arts. He pays the writer generously, suggests
ideas to him, invites him to lunch, meets him in the
city for cocktails, and gives him his home telephone number, which is unlisted. If an article by
his current favorite appears in another magazine,
Wallace sends him a note complimenting him on
the piece and asking wistfully why he didn't write
it for the *Digest*. A Wallace enthusiasm for a
writer ends abruptly and without formal notice.
The author merely stops hearing from him. If the
writer phones or happens to meet Wallace, the

patron is polite and pleasant but rather distant, as though he didn't quite catch the name.

Until a few years ago, Wallace owned a rather modest house on Grandview Avenue, in Pleasant-ville, the town which is next to Chappaqua and in which the *Digest* formerly had its offices. This was Wallace's official residence, but how much the Wal-laces actually lived in it is a matter that still starts debates in Pleasantville. When Wallace invited editors from the city to dine with him, they were entertained there, comfortably but not preten-tiously, under the ministrations of a Japanese butler named Yama. However, the Wallaces sup-posedly spent much of their time in what knowl-edgeable people called their "secret house," a Norman-style, six-bedroom hideaway several miles distant. It was approached by turning off a highway and driving across a field, or anyhow that was *one* way of getting to it. It sat concealed in a clearing surrounded by high trees, and it satisfied the longing, which Wallace often feels, to be alone.

The house in which the Wallaces live today, though less secluded than their woodland dwell-ing, is still about as accessible as Fort Knox. It is set high on a wooded bluff overlooking Byram

Lake, in Mount Kisco. Many local residents refer to the place as The Castle. It has gleaming walls, many chimneys, a cobalt-blue slate roof, and, as its most prominent feature, a circular, peaked turret. The architecture is reminiscent of the castle in Walt Disney's *Snow White*. It has three stories and twenty-four rooms. The building and the plot of a hundred and five acres of farm and wooded land which surround it are assessed at $177,000. The interior, done by Mrs. Wallace, whose hobby is decorating, is generally considered elegant by their infrequent visitors. In these regal surroundings, Wallace and his wife, who are childless, live rather simply. Their dinner guests are mostly relatives or business acquaintances, including high-ranking *Digest* editors and executives. The Wallaces have on occasion entertained nobility. The Duke and Duchess of Windsor have been luncheon guests, and Lord Halifax has come to call. The Empire is evidently not unaware that the sun never sets on readers of the *Digest*.

Mrs. Wallace, a quietly confident woman, both as hostess and as journalist, is the daughter of a Presbyterian minister. She is small, mentally

adroit, stylish, and eager. From the beginning, she
has been listed on the *Digest's* masthead as an
editor, and Wallace is never niggardly in estimat-
ing her contribution to its success. She no longer
has an office in the *Digest* building, but her contin-
uing influence on the magazine is not minimized by
Digest people. She takes a matriarchal interest in
the employees and occasionally invites some of
them, on the medium and higher editorial levels,
to lunch, at which she pleasantly inquires into
their affairs and assures them of the company's
wish to make all its help happy. Mrs. Wallace was
instrumental in organizing the Reader's Digest
Players, an amateur theatrical group composed of
employees, whose repertoire features some of the
works of Dorothy Parker and Noel Coward, in
addition to monologues of a humorous nature
written by *Digest* workers. She likes to ride and to
read full-length books, pursuits in which her husband rarely joins her. She frequently spends a few
days in town, shopping, visiting her hairdresser,
and going to matinées. Once in a while she prevails
upon Wallace to come into town with her to go to
the theater or, more rarely, to go tea dancing at
the Plaza. Wallace dances with the expertness of a

man who has received professional instruction, but he has only a passive interest in the art.

The only diversion that has ever wooed Wallace away from work, with the mild exception of poker, is flying. Before the war he sometimes gathered up a bundle of manuscripts and took long trips on commercial airliners, excising as he flew. In the late thirties, Wallace, who was not completely satisfied with commercial planes because, he said, they flew too high to afford a good view of the countryside, bought a four-passenger Fairchild, and learned to fly it. After getting a pilot's license, he spent many happy, solitary hours cruising around at two thousand feet, the altitude he found best for reconnaissance. He occasionally left his office, drove over to the Armonk airport, where he kept his plane, and flew away without leaving word at the *Digest* where he could be reached, or even that he was taking off. Once, a writer, meeting a *Digest* editor in New York, remarked that he had received a nice note from Wallace that morning about a piece he had submitted. "Good grief!" the editor exclaimed. "Where is he? We've been looking all over for him." It developed that Wallace had flown to a resort town in the Poconos to spend a few quiet days with his manuscripts. Another time, not bothering to take his plane, he dropped out of sight again. A few days later, the *Digest* discovered that he was in Hawaii with Mrs. Wallace. He went on from there to India. From time to time he cabled home decisions on several articles he had taken to read en route. In September, 1940, he gave his plane to the Royal Canadian Air Force, a gesture perhaps prompted by the appearance in the *Digest* the same month of an article by Robert E. Sherwood entitled "Rush All Possible Aid to Britain!" Wallace, who had to give up sudden long-distance travel soon after the war broke out and has not yet resumed it, still disappears from his office, but lately he has seldom strayed farther than New York. Secluding himself at the Roosevelt, Plaza, or Hampshire House, he spends a couple of days working alone in his room. When he tires of this, he phones one of the regular contributors to the *Digest* and invites him to come over and pass the time of day. One afternoon, while chatting with an author who never writes on political topics, he said abruptly, "Why don't you go over to the Waldorf Towers and have a talk with Herbert Hoover?"

"What for, Wally?" his companion asked. "What's the story?" "Oh, no story, I guess," Wallace said. "I was just thinking, Hoover's probably sitting over there all by himself with nobody to talk to. I'll bet he's lonesome."

That no man, even an ex-President, can live by bread alone is a precept in which Wallace has implicit faith, as nearly everyone who meets him quickly discovers. "I came away greatly impressed," the Duke of Windsor said after lunching with Wallace, "by the profoundly practical idealism which has guided *The Reader's Digest* since its inception." He should have been. When Wallace founded the *Digest,* twenty-four years ago, he innocently hoped that it would provide him and his wife with an income of five thousand a year. It was not a great while, as such things go, before the little magazine was bringing them an income of more than a hundred times that. As a practical idealist, Wallace found this distressing. A large income is apparently as depressing to him as a long article: he must get rid of as much as he can of both to be happy. Fortunately, he has been able to find a considerable number of people willing to help him out, among them his business associates and his fifty-two editors. Kenneth W. Payne, his executive editor, for instance, has co-operated to the extent of unburdening him of about a million dollars in the past ten years, and the others have done the best they could. Wallace once had an argument with the state tax authorities about the salaries and bonuses he was paying. A state tax man declared that his employees couldn't possibly, as a matter of plain common sense, be worth as much as Wallace was paying them. Wallace talked the tax man down on that.

The federal government, of course, put a rather discouraging limit to the amount Wallace could palm off on his employees during the war, but on one occasion the War Labor Board turned out to be a peculiarly helpful agency in holding down the Wallace income. In 1943, before Christmas, Wallace worked out a new scheme for paying bonuses to the part-time employees who are hired annually to handle the holiday subscription rush. The new plan had the virtue of relieving Wallace of several thousand dollars more than the one used the year before, but the W.L.B. failed to give it full approval. That didn't defeat Wallace. He had solved the problem in advance by paying the bonuses first and then sending his lawyers to the board to report what he had done. The lawyers returned with the cheerful news that he could dispose of approximately fifty thousand dollars more as a penalty. Wallace was undoubtedly grateful for the government's assistance, but in general he doesn't believe in putting too much strain on the Secretary of the Treasury and feels that his relatives ought to share a little of the burden. Thirty-two of them are the beneficiaries of a trust fund the Wallaces created for them some years ago, and they do their bit by pocketing about thirty thousand a year.

In his struggle to disengage himself from his wealth, Wallace is about as unevenly matched as King Midas. The *Digest* makes more money with every passing year, and Wallace and his wife own all the common stock. Wallace owns fifty-two per cent and Mrs. Wallace forty-eight per cent. In 1939, when life and taxes were simpler, Wallace's personal income was $286,011 and his wife's $254,816, or $540,827 together. These figures impress Wallace's colleagues in the publishing business not because they are so large but because they are so small. They indicate that Wallace's plucky fight to keep his income in check has been pretty successful. However, this has taken super-financing. The publishing people figure that it costs about four cents, or a little more, to manufacture a copy of the *Digest*—that is, to pay for the paper, printing, and ink—and presumably Wallace nets about fourteen or fifteen cents a copy, whether from newsstand sales or subscriptions. That leaves a spread of ten cents a copy, or around ten million dollars a year, for business and editorial expenses, corporation taxes, and, God forbid, dividends. It is easy to see what Wallace is up against.

2

BIRTH OF AN ARISTOCRAT

THE autobiographical sketch which DeWitt Wallace contributed to the current edition of *Who's Who* is a fair specimen of Wallace's dazzling talent for condensation. Wallace, one of the influential men of our time and one of the most successful editors of all time, squeezed his entire career into nine lines of *Who's Who* type. In making a mountain into a molehill, Wallace has no peer. None of the eighteen subordinate *Digest* editors who are listed in *Who's Who* abridged himself as brilliantly as the master. Henry Luce and William Randolph Hearst, mighty editors with whom Wallace is sometimes compared, both took more than twice as much space to carry on about themselves. Like most condensations, however, Wallace's biographical tour de force had lost something in the cutting room. In compressing himself, Wallace left out a few not altogether inconsequential items, such as his full name and his age. According to a journal kept by his father, the late Dr. James Wallace, DeWitt was born in St. Paul on November 12, 1889. "My wife," the elder Wallace recorded in this informal family history, "named him William Roy, to which I added DeWitt in honor of my cousin, DeWitt Wallace, of Lafayette, Indiana." Wallace sensed a superfluity in his name at an early age and began trimming it down, first excising William and then Roy. He has always been listed on his magazine's masthead simply as De-Witt Wallace. Although most of his upper-bracket co-workers accomplish a further reduction by calling him Wally, neither Wallace nor any of his editorial helpers has had as much success in condensing the name of their magazine, beyond the rather obvious truncation to the *Digest*. Some research toward working out a further abbreviation has been done, however, by a brisk New York radio man, who refers to the magazine simply as the *Jest*.

Although Wallace enjoys having a hearty laugh now and then, he does not find this condensation as diverting as his father, the late Dr. Wallace, might have. The Doctor was a scholar of Greek and Latin, a staunch churchman, and president of Macalester College, a small Presbyterian institution in St. Paul, but he had a taste for lambent humor and was not averse to getting off modest, though at times severely academic, witticisms. Comparing the merits of Greek and football—a game he liked but had intellectual reservations about—in a newspaper interview on his ninetieth birthday, in 1939, he said, "There is too much 'sock' and not enough Socrates in college life today. I am afraid that there is a danger of our century's athletics going the way they did in ancient Greece, when they were developed to a point where they became a thorough abuse. Epaminondas, you know, drummed the athletes out of his army." The idea of dehydrating literature into pellets to be taken one a day, like vitamin pills, never appealed to Dr. Wallace. He took his literature whole. His interest in contemporary writing, even in its undigested state, was not excessive. "Do you know," he said to a friend when he was eighty-four, "that I haven't read more than ten of the modern novelists—Scott, Dickens, and the rest? Sounds a bit funny, doesn't it, for a man who is supposed to be educated?'' Dr. Wallace was as intimate with the works of Xenophon as his son is with the shorter works of Louis Bromfield; he often carried on a conversation with a colleague in Greek and thought nothing of composing a letter in Latin. Admired on the Macalester campus for his lively interest in athletics as well as for his learning, he amused the college when he was eighty-nine by riding in a Homecoming Day parade in the rumble seat of a roadster, flanked by pretty girls. When later he was asked about the experience, he remarked, ''The proximity of my pleasant companions was delightful.''

An oil portrait of Dr. Wallace, which the editor of the *Digest* commissioned and presented to Macalester College, hangs in the office of its present president. The picture indicates that while the Doctor may have had his little jokes, he was by no means a comedian. He is shown seated, a spare, sturdy, gray-bearded man, impressive in his academic robes. The likeness seems to support the description of a colleague, who said, ''He was an Old Testament crusader.'' Dr. Wallace was the son of strict Scotch-Irish Presbyterian parents. He was reared on an Ohio farm and nourished, as a faculty associate once remarked, "on liberal portions of the Scripture and the Westminster Shorter Catechism along with his oatmeal porridge." He graduated from Wooster College, as valedictorian, in 1874 and married the daughter of a Presbyterian minister. When he arrived in St. Paul in the late eighties to become professor of Greek and of Early English Literature at Macalester College, the institution consisted of one building sitting on the edge of a cornfield. During the depression of 1894, when the trustees were almost ready to give up and close the college, Dr. Wallace was made president, talked half a dozen professors into serving without pay, and saved the day. When he resigned the presidency, twelve years later, and resumed teaching, as head of the Biblical department, he had paid off a debt of $125,000 for the college and got it on a sound financial footing. In 1932, after having received a Doctor of Divinity degree and having been president emeritus for several years, he retired to devote his time to study, writing, and what he called "the luxury of making speeches." He was a resolute believer in international coöperation, and wrote and spoke fervently in defense of the League of

Nations and the World Court. He once said that
their failure was the greatest disappointment of
his life. Just as he is remembered as the Grand
Old Man of Macalester College, so his son DeWitt
is today honored as its Grand Middle-Aged Man.
On the wall of the president's office there hangs,
near Dr. Wallace's portrait, a small photograph of
the editor of *The Reader's Digest,* who has made
gifts to the college totaling three hundred thousand dollars.

During his first twenty years, DeWitt Wallace
lived about as close to learning as it is possible to
get, for the family home was a large frame house
on a corner of the Macalester campus. He was the
second youngest of five children, two girls and
three boys. His mother was a demure, unusually
quiet, well-educated woman. Some elderly friends
of the family say that the *Digest* editor resembles
his mother, but they also recall that DeWitt, when
he was a child with curly hair down to his shoulders, was "a gay, bright, spicy little fellow." The
Wallace living room was a gathering place for
the children of the neighborhood, and batches of
them used to stay to lunch. A large map of the

United States hung on a wall of the dining room, and, after saying grace, Dr. Wallace occasionally announced, "Children, I think you ought to know more about your country," and spent the lunchtime telling them the complete history of some one of the states. DeWitt attended public school and spent his vacations at the family's summer place in Wisconsin. It was at the summer residence, in 1920, six years after DeWitt's mother died, that Dr. Wallace remarried, at the age of seventy-one. His bride, who was fifty-eight, was his first wife's sister. DeWitt and the other Wallace children were fond of their stepmother, whom they continued to call Aunt Miriam. In 1933, when Dr. Wallace and his wife returned to St. Paul from a winter in California, DeWitt met the elderly couple at the railroad station and drove them to a new twelve-thousand-dollar bungalow he had secretly bought and furnished for them. The Doctor lived in the house until his death, at the age of ninety.

All of Dr. Wallace's children were expected to go to Macalester College, and all did. By the time DeWitt enrolled, in 1907, his two brothers and one of his sisters had already been there and set a stiff scholastic pace. Benjamin, the oldest of the children, who is like Dr. Wallace in appearance and temperament, was the first Rhodes Scholar appointed from Minnesota. He later got a Ph.D. from the University of Wisconsin and is now Special Adviser in the United States Tariff Commission in Washington. DeWitt's other brother, Robert, after graduating from Macalester and studying agriculture and forestry abroad, became an experimental farmer. Today he spends part of his time on a farm in Wisconsin and part at his home in St. Paul. DeWitt's sisters were married after finishing college, one of them to a minister, the other to an electrical engineer. At Macalester, DeWitt played second base on the baseball team, clerked for a while in the campus bookstore, and never became engrossed in his studies. After two years, he transferred to the University of California, in order to join two of his boyhood friends. By that time he had given up all notion of becoming a scholar, so, to make the academic burden as light as possible, he enrolled for the second time as a freshman. After working up to being a sophomore again, he gave up schooling.

Wallace returned to St. Paul and got a job with

the Webb Publishing Company, which issues farm magazines and textbooks used in agricultural schools. He handled the correspondence in the book department. "Oh, that boy could write a fine letter," an associate there has recalled, "but he was restless—like a bird in a cage, always looking out." What Wallace was looking out at, at least during his latter days with the Webb company, was visions of a little magazine that would reprint articles from other magazines in condensed form and carry no advertising. The idea for such a publication had occurred to him as he went about his duties. He discussed it with two or three of his office acquaintances. Their responses were discouraging but they didn't seem to make Wallace downcast. One day when he was twenty-six and had been with the Webb company four years, without making noticeable progress, he walked into the office of one of the owners and handed him a list of mistakes he considered that his superior, the head of the agricultural-books department, had made in the past year. The publisher read its several pages as Wallace waited, and said, "This is an interesting document, De-Witt. I'm sorry it means you're fired. We don't believe in this sort of thing.'' Wallace, shocked, said he was just trying to be helpful, and it was obvious to the publisher that his intentions were honorable. The publisher was willing to regard the affair as a youthful indiscretion, but he didn't go as far as to rescind the discharge order. He extended Wallace printing credit up to seven hundred dollars, so that he could get started in business for himself. Wallace spent the next several months compiling and selling a pamphlet that listed the publications issued by the federal and state Departments of Agriculture. He sold these pamphlets in lots to small-town banks, feed stores, and such, which gave them away to their customers. He wound up his first publishing venture with enough cash to pay his printing bill.

Wallace spent the next year as a salesman for Brown & Bigelow, St. Paul calendar printers, and then, in September, 1917, entered the Army as a private. Arriving in France in late spring of the following year as an infantryman in the Thirty-fifth Division, he fought through that crucial summer and became a sergeant. During the Meuse-Argonne offensive, he was hit by shrapnel in the neck, back, and shoulders. He was hospitalized for three months, during much of which he practiced pruning magazine articles. He found, as he had long suspected, that they could easily be reduced in length. He continued these experiments after he came home and was discharged from the Army in May, 1919, and during the six months he spent in Pittsburgh, in the foreign-publicity department of the Westinghouse Electric Company, where his brother Benjamin was then employed. When Westinghouse cut down on publicity, Wallace, the last hired, was the first fired. Exasperated by the fickleness of industry, he began work on a prospectus for the magazine he had decided to call *The Reader's Digest*. He put the bee on brother Benjamin for three hundred dollars to help finance this preparatory work and went to his father for a little more money. Like nearly everyone else DeWitt had spoken to about his idea, Wallace Senior wasn't sanguine. DeWitt, however, was completely confident. "We're living in a fast-moving world," he told his father. "People are anxious to get at the nub of matters." To help his boy get at the nub, Dr. Wallace matched Ben's loan, but not without misgivings. He reminded DeWitt that he had never been very good at English.

Perhaps the only person, aside from DeWitt, who was completely enthusiastic about the *Digest* idea was his fiancée, Miss Lila Bell Acheson, who, like his mother, was the daughter of a Presbyterian minister. She was an attractive, ambitious, and capable girl, who had been born in Virden, Manitoba, and had grown up in Seattle. Wallace had met her while spending a Christmas vacation at her family's home with her brother Barclay, who was also attending Macalester. The three young people continued their friendship by correspondence through the war, during which Barclay was secretary of the Y.M.C.A. in Portland, Oregon, and Lila traveled about the country with her parents doing morale work in war plants for the Presbyterian Church. After the war, she and her brother, who eventually became a Presbyterian minister and is now the *Digest's* Director of International Editions, went to Constantinople to work for the Near East Relief. She returned in 1921 and in New York met Wallace, who was struggling with the problem of starting his little journal for a fast-moving world. They became engaged and they became co-editors, both of them unhampered by previous journalistic experience. They opened an office in a basement storeroom they rented at 1 Minetta Lane, in Greenwich Village, and spent the summer clipping out, carving up, dissecting, and suturing magazine pieces and preparing a mimeographed circular to solicit subscriptions. The Reader's Digest Association was established in the early fall. On October 15, the co-editors were married. That same day, they dropped thousands of their prospectuses in the mail and left town on a brief honeymoon. When they returned, they found, to their amazement, fifteen hundred charter subscriptions, accompanied by three dollars each. Thus provided with forty-five hundred dollars in cash, they set to work making up the first issue. Dated February, 1922, Vol. 1, No. 1 of *The Reader's Digest* carried on its masthead the wildly unprophetic legend "The Little Magazine."

The honor of being responsible for the first piece of editorial matter in the first issue of the *Digest* belongs to a venerable woman journalist and maker of epigrams named Helen Rowland. Her contribution, which led off a department called "Remarkable Remarks," read, "From the day on which she tips the scales at 140 the chief excitement of a woman's life consists in spotting women who are fatter than she is." Miss Rowland's place in magazine history is likely to be a trifle uneasy, however, as the *Digest,* making the least of its first opportunity to get something right, misspelled her name. The epigram was attributed to one Helen Howland. The editors had better luck in identifying the authors of the other snappy quotations in this collection, which included John Wanamaker's "A real good smile and a hearty handshake cost but a minute" and Billy Sunday's "Try praising your wife, even if it does frighten her at first." This department also launched the *Digest's* anticigarette crusade with a remarkable remark by Homer Rodeheaver, Billy Sunday's trombone player, who said starkly, and it would seem somewhat cryptically, "One cigarette will kill a cat." The lead article in the first issue of the *Digest* was entitled "How to Keep Young Mentally." It was a condensation of an interview with Alexander Graham Bell, on self-education, that had appeared in the *American Magazine.* The historic first paragraph began:

Alexander Graham Bell, the famous scientist and inventor, will be seventy-four years old in March. Yet an acquaintance said, "The most remarkable thing about Dr. Bell is that he is younger, in mind, than most men of half his age. Mentally, he seems to have discovered a Fountain of Youth, which keeps him perennially alert and vigorous."

The article then quoted Dr. Bell:

I have given the subject of self-education a great deal of thought and have evolved what you might call a "Rule of Three" in regard to it. The rule is simply this: Observe! Remember! Compare! . . . Remember what you have observed. Compare the facts you have observed; and you will find yourself thinking out conclusions.

Applying Dr. Bell's rule to the contents of the first issue, a reader might find himself thinking out the conclusion that the *Digest* had small chance of reaching a circulation of eleven thousand, let alone eleven million. The first issue was typographically inept and editorially unimpressive. It seemed to be aimed chiefly at feminine readers, which was intentional. In appraising their market, the Wallaces had erroneously figured that a journal of the sort they were putting out would appeal more to women than to men. Accordingly, their cover design showed a woman writing on a scroll with an immense quill pen and their masthead listed Lila Bell Acheson, DeWitt Wallace, Louise M. Patterson, and Hazel J. Cubberley as the editors, in that order. The last two were relatives whose names were solely window dressing. Of the thirty-one articles in the first issue, many, such as "Wanted—Motives for Motherhood," "Untying the Apron Strings," and "Love—Luxury or Necessity?," were clearly designed for restless housewives. There were, of course, some more masculine stories, such as "The Future of Poison Gas" and "Printing and Its Early Vicissitudes." The pioneer issue finished with an article challengingly titled "Don't Growl—Kick." This advised readers who were upset by the actions of a big corporation to drop it a note. "Corporations really have souls," the article ended cheerily. "The system is much better than the average fellows knows, and somebody is probably waiting to attend him in this very matter."

Despite its amateurishness and signs of stage-fright, the first issue was a hit. The second number contained a folksy message from Lila Bell Acheson saying that it had been "successful beyond all anticipations." A few issues later, in a pep talk urging the readers to help out by getting their friends to enter subscriptions, she promised them that "when our present circulation is doubled, the *Digest* will appear with a cover so attractive that it will be truly THE LITTLE ARISTOCRAT among periodicals—in both appearance and content." When, a couple of years later, The Little Aristocrat appeared with a heavy paper cover on which the index was printed, it began to look, in most of its essentials, like The Big Aristocrat of today. The tone was set. What appealed to a few thousand readers then appeals to eleven million readers now. A representative collection of articles from the early issues might easily appear in the *Digest* today: "The Art of Opening a Conversation," "Three Suggestions to Insure Your Happiness," "The Menace of the Polish Jew," "Religion as an Adventure," "Russia Ended Socialism for Me," "The Strange Life of the Salmon," "Wasteful Regulations of Labor Unions," "Sex in American

Literature," "America for the Americans," and "Charley Ross, the Unforgotten Lost Boy." From the beginning, the *Digest* was popular with the clergy. Henry Luce's father, a missionary, endorsed it. "In its field," he wrote from Peking, "the *Digest* helps as much as *Time* does in its field." Most of the praise from lay readers, on the other hand, was not qualified. An educated admirer in West Newton, Pennsylvania, confessing that he couldn't find an English word good enough to describe the *Digest*, said, "The French have the word, '*magnifique.*' "

Having accumulated a small surplus by the end of the first year, Wallace and his co-editor decided to desert Greenwich Village, where conditions for producing a magazine with ecclesiastical overtones were not, they considered, ideal. By following up a newspaper advertisement, they found new quarters on an estate in peaceful Pleasantville, forty miles north of the city. The estate was owned by Pendleton Dudley, a New York publicity counsellor who took an avuncular interest in the striving journalists and has since become an intimate friend and adviser. For three years, the *Digest* editors lived and worked in two rooms over Dudley's garage, while three girls, hired to handle subscriptions and do other routine chores, worked in his pony shed. In 1926, Wallace bought property next to Dudley's and built a house designed to serve as a combination residence and office. By this time, the circulation of the *Digest* had reached twenty thousand. The diminutive aristocrat was now bringing in an annual gross income of around sixty thousand dollars.

Aside from the cost of subscriptions to a number of periodicals and an occasional investment in a new pair of scissors, the *Digest's* overhead was small, and its content was obtained, with surprising ease, free of charge. Wallace made occasional trips to the city, called on the editors and business managers of magazines, shyly complimented them on certain articles they had published, and asked permission to reprint them. He was rarely refused. A few of these magazine people recall that they were not quite sure what Wallace was up to, but most of them saw no harm in letting him use their stuff second-hand, though they were sometimes too busy to make the presentation in person. "We figured he was just another guy with a crackpot idea," one editor has said in explaining why he now and then turned the task of dealing with Wallace over to a stenographer who didn't have too much to do. As the *Digest's* popularity grew, publishers and editors generally were willing to let Wallace reprint from their magazines without paying because they felt, as many of them still do, that appearing in the *Digest* had great promotional value. "Back in the late twenties," the editor of a substantial monthly magazine has said, "we used to think that getting one of our pieces into *The Reader's Digest* was like making the All-American."

Not every publisher and editor felt this sense of glory. Some of them regarded the *Digest* as a parasitic enterprise and potential competitor and couldn't see why they should support it. In 1929, when it became known, despite Wallace's extreme secrecy about his magazine's circulation, that the *Digest* had 290,000 readers, *Scribner's* withdrew its permission to reprint and several other magazines, including *Forum* and the *Atlantic Monthly*, began to consider breaking off relations. In countering this threat, Wallace had some help from Kenneth W. Payne, then editor of the *North American Review*. Payne liked the *Digest*, and when he discussed the publication with his friends on other magazines, which he did rather incessantly, he argued that the *Digest* did not cut into their circulation but actually aided it by encouraging a wider interest in reading. Payne, as Wallace's busy advocate, was so successful that none of the vacillating magazines renounced the *Digest* and *Scribner's* eventually returned to the fold. Not long after accomplishing this impressive missionary work, Payne took the final vows. In the January, 1931, issue of the *Digest,* his name appeared in the list of editors. This was in the period of the *Digest's* first great upswing, and within three years Wallace was rewarding him with an annual income of $102,467.

While quelling the rebellion, Wallace was also taking steps to deal with an assortment of competitive reprint magazines that had begun appearing toward the end of the twenties. These imitated the *Digest's* format and technique and sold briskly on the newsstands, where they had no competition from the *Digest*, which was still being sold only by subscription. Distributing agencies had asked Wallace to let them put the *Digest* on the newsstands, but he had refused because of a mistaken notion that his magazine was too aristocratic for popular consumption. The success of his imitators changed his mind, and in 1929 he made a deal with the S-M News Company, an affiliate of the McCall Corporation, to handle the *Digest* on the stands. The first year, newsstand sales averaged 106,000 copies a month. Next, Wallace proposed to most of the larger magazines that they enter into an agreement giving the *Digest* exclusive magazine reprint rights, in return for a modest sum, in the neighborhood of fifty dollars, for each article used. With the exception of the *Saturday Evening Post* and the *American*, both of which later joined the parade, all the big magazines promptly accepted Wallace's offer. Partly as a hedge against the day they might change their minds and partly because he felt an uncontrollable urge to branch out as a creative editor, Wallace also hired several men whom he arbitrarily designated "editors" and put them to work writing articles. These authors were prolific workers, and their output subsequently came to account for a sizable portion of the *Digest's* content.

With his present staff of fifty-two editors, some

of whom actually *are* editors, Wallace could, if his sources of reprint supply should ever dry up, undoubtedly continue to fill his magazine, as well as three or four other magazines, entirely with articles written in his own organization. To avoid having to make such a flagrant departure from his original publishing concept, Wallace is assiduous in his efforts to keep the *Digest's* reprint contacts in good order. He trusts the handling of this integral part of the business to no one but himself. A few magazines, including *Cosmopolitan, Good Housekeeping,* the *New Republic,* the *Nation,* and the *New Yorker,* have in recent times refused to renew their contracts, but Wallace has kept the other magazines in line. At present the *Digest* has reprint agreements with some forty periodicals. Wallace's constituency includes most of the large-circulation weeklies, such as the *Saturday Evening Post, Life, Collier's, Liberty,* and *Time*; such monthlies as *Harper's, Redbook, Esquire, Fortune,* the *Atlantic,* and the *American Mercury*; and an assortment of other publications, such as the *Saturday Review of Literature,* the *Rotarian,* and *Survey Graphic.* As a rule, *Digest* contracts run for three years.

They now provide for the payment of a flat annual fee for the privilege of reprinting up to twenty articles a year, and a further payment if additional articles are used. As a precaution against the embarrassment resulting from a simultaneous mass withdrawal of his constituents, Wallace has staggered the expiration dates of his contracts. A few weeks before one is to expire, Wallace arranges to lunch with one of the officials of the magazine involved to discuss a renewal. He usually comes with glad financial tidings, for as the *Digest's* circulation has grown, he has steadily increased the payments to his supporting magazines. The fees were sharply advanced when, in 1936, *Fortune* disclosed that the *Digest's* circulation, which rumors from Pleasantville had placed at around 750,000, had actually risen to 1,800,000. Wallace is now as secretive about his contracts as he once was about his circulation figures, but people who get around in the publishing business report that the *Digest's* annual payments to magazines begin at around $3,500 to the *Saturday Review of Literature*. The fees range thence upward to $18,000 or thereabouts, paid to the *American Mercury*, and $35,000, to the Luce publications

46-963

combined, and reach their peak with the Crowell and Curtis publishing companies, which receive $50,000 each. Besides compensating the magazines, Wallace also rewards the authors of reprinted articles by paying them at the rate of $150 per *Digest* page. Under the Wallace system, apparently, everybody wins.

For some small periodicals, a handout from the *Digest* could mean the difference between existence and disappearance, but for a successful publishing enterprise like the Luce Empire, whose income runs into millions of dollars, the *Digest's* donation is insignificant. However small, it seems to be welcomed everywhere. It has the irresistible fascination of free money. After making some rather comprehensive criticisms of the *Digest,* the editor of an old and respected magazine once said that his business office is nevertheless always pleased to take Wallace's cash. "To turn it down," he added, "would be as foolish as refusing a legacy from your uncle because you never liked the way the old gentleman combed his hair." This practical editor feels the way many of his colleagues do—that they invested in Wallace when they let him use their articles and that the money he now distributes is in the nature of dividends. With some reason, they feel they helped make Wallace what he is today, and by and large they seem quite satisfied.

3

PLANT YOU NOW, DIG YOU LATER

WHEN DeWitt Wallace established *The Reader's Digest,* he summed up the aim of his magazine in a slogan: "An article a day from leading magazines, in condensed, permanent booklet form." This slogan, reminiscent of Dr. Eliot's Five Foot Shelf and other short cuts to culture, was printed on the first page of every issue of *The Reader's Digest* from August, 1923, through May, 1939. In the issue of June, 1939, the motto was quietly altered. Wallace deleted the phrase "from leading magazines" and substituted the less reassuring phrase "of enduring significance." To many people in the publishing business, this change was more amusing than surprising; it seemed to them long overdue. For years, the fact that *The Reader's Digest* had ceased to be solely a reprint magazine had, to its devoted students, been as obvious as the falseness of Groucho Marx's mustache. By millions of less analytical readers, however, the *Digest's* metamorphosis has as yet apparently never been noticed. It is evidently as hard for a *Digest* fan to think of his favorite magazine as anything but a regurgitative journal as it would be for a clean-shaven Groucho to stalk Mrs. Rittenhouse. The *Digest* has not exerted itself immoderately to shatter the illusion. A year after acknowledging, by implication, the changed character of his magazine, Wallace printed a warm testimonial to it by John Kieran, the amiable permanent expert of "Information, Please!" Kieran, paraphrasing the chant of millions of other *Digest* devotees—"I don't have time to read *all* the magazines, so I just read the *best* from all of them in the little magazine that fits right into my pocket"—said that the *Digest* performed a great service for him by sifting the best articles from the "vast flood of contemporary letters. It is the one periodical I read regularly, knowing that in it I will get the best sum and substance of today's literary output." Kieran ended, not unexpectedly, with a quotation from *Hamlet*: "For this relief, much thanks." Alas, poor Kieran! He did not know the *Digest* well.

The transformation of *The Reader's Digest* into something other than a digest began in the early thirties. Among other things, it was a maneuver of self-defense. A small rebellion against the *Digest* had broken out among a group of strong-minded publishers and editors, who considered denying the *Digest* the privilege of reprinting articles from their magazines. Threatened with the possible loss of his sources of supply, Wallace countered by hiring a few men to write articles directly for the *Digest*. The rebellion petered out, but Wallace, perhaps expecting another one later on, continued to build up his defenses by having his writers turn out more and more material. In June, 1930, he began publishing occasional articles that were on the borderline between reprints and originals. These, it was announced in the *Digest*, were based on articles that had appeared in other publications. The magazines were not identified and the articles, written by Wallace's staff authors, were anonymous. These articles, presented under a rather evasive editorial note reading, "It was felt that on this subject, the interest of our readers is best served by this summary, specially prepared by one of our editors," bore such arresting titles as "Music and Animals" and "Why Be Bald?" Wallace continued to serve the best interests of his readers with similar summaries until February, 1933, when he at last decided to publish the first admittedly original article. This historic contribution was written, and signed, by Henry Morton Robinson, at present a Roving Editor of the *Digest*, and was entitled "Insanity—The Modern Menace." There were fourteen other original articles in the *Digest* that year, none of which seemed to charm its readers more than a piece called "The Burning Question," an article about cremation.

Until 1935, Wallace may reasonably have wondered whether he hadn't made a mistake in going into the intricate business of manufacturing articles instead of simply reprocessing old ones. As far as anyone could tell, the customers seemed to like the reused goods as well as the new. He nevertheless kept offering more samples, and of the forty originals he printed that year, one turned out to be a startling success. This was a sanguinary piece about automobile accidents called

"—And Sudden Death," written by J. C. Furnas. It turned out to be the most widely read magazine article ever published anywhere. Wallace got the idea when, as he was speeding through the countryside near Pleasantville one spring afternoon, a tire on his car blew out. At the garage where he had it repaired, he fell into conversation with an articulate mechanic, who recited several blood-curdling accounts of automobile wrecks he had seen. Wallace was impressed. He quickly got in touch with Furnas, who was working on a *Digest* article about traffic problems, and told him to drop it and immediately start doing a short but vivid article that would shock the nation into realizing that careful driving was essential. Bearing a title taken from the Book of Common Prayer, Furnas's story, full of "raw ends of bones protruding through flesh," "dark red, oozing surfaces," and corpses, was published in the August issue.

The week the article appeared, the *Digest* sent proofs of it to five thousand newspapers and other publications and invited them to reprint it. Almost all did. In several Hearst dailies, Arthur Brisbane's column was pushed off Page 1 to make room for the gory treatise. Within a few weeks, it had been reprinted in whole or in part by newspapers in every large American city, and in hundreds of weeklies, farm and religious journals, college magazines, and house organs. In addition, it was read or discussed on numerous radio programs, read aloud at dozens of Rotary and Kiwanis gatherings, syndicated in comic-strip form, and made into a movie short. A traffic-court judge in New York opened proceedings every morning by reading it to his audience, other magistrates made offenders copy it in longhand, the State of Wyoming mailed a reprint of it with every set of license plates, the Port of New York Authority had reprints handed to motorists going through the Holland Tunnel or over the George Washington Bridge, and a reprint was sent out with all official correspondence of the Province of Ontario. For a while, the article had a marked effect on the journalistic approach to reporting automobile accidents. It got so a routine newspaper story about a smashup read like an account of a journey through a slaughterhouse with pad and pencil. Within three months after the article had appeared, four million reprints had been shipped off to the more than eight thousand business concerns, clubs, and other organizations that had requested them. The reprints, it was announced, were distributed as a public service, for, as the *Digest* remarked, with more good will than good grammar, "Convinced that widespread reading of this article will help curb reckless driving, reprints in leaflet form are offered at cost." What effect the extensive distribution of this gruesome work of art had on reckless driving is hard to say with certainty, but it may be significant that in 1936, the year after it came out, 1,720 more persons were killed in automobile accidents in this country than the year before, and the figure rose even higher the next year.

Whatever the practical results of the Furnas article, the effect on Wallace was exhilarating. It bolstered his confidence in his editorial judgment, and it provided an excellent retort to the editors of other magazines who had got into the habit of patronizingly calling him "the world's greatest second-guess editor." In thirteen years as a publisher, Wallace had reprinted hundreds of articles published by other editors and not one had been half as sensational as a piece he thought up by himself while hanging around in a country garage.

Since it seemed clear that his hunches about what people want to read were as good as or better than those of any of his colleagues, and since he was also suffering from a combined creative and evangelical itch, Wallace determined to become a permanent first-guess editor. To do this overtly, he was aware, would bring up a perplexing publishing problem, for if the *Digest* began appearing with large numbers of frankly original articles, many readers like John Kieran might get the impression that their favorite periodical was no longer providing them with an accurate cross-section of the best sum and substance of the current literary output. Wallace solved the problem by inventing the "planted" article—perhaps the most important journalistic innovation since the invention of the digest magazine itself. A *Digest* "plant" is the same as a *Digest* original, with one exception. Both plants and originals are planned, assigned to authors, and paid for by the *Digest*. The original articles are published in the *Digest* without being ascribed to any other magazine. Before a plant appears in the *Digest*, however, it is sent to some other periodical; say, the *Rotarian*. The *Rotarian* publishes the article. The *Digest* then "reprints" it, under a line saying "Condensed from *The Rotarian*." The advantages of the planting system to Wallace are obvious; it allows him to have the fun of being a first-guess editor and at the same time to observe the letter, if not the precise spirit, of what is expected of a reprint magazine.

For some reason, Wallace has always been something less than garrulous about the extent of the *Digest's* planting activities. People who have been interested enough to ask the *Digest* how much of the magazine's content is supplied by other periodicals and how much is originated by the *Digest* have received responses in straight-from-the-shoulder double talk. However, an irrepressible statistician named George W. Bennett recently knocked himself out getting up some figures and arrived at a reasonably accurate answer to this question. During the five years from 1939 through 1943, the *Digest* printed 1,908 articles of one page or more in length, not including the book section or such filler items as "Picturesque Speech and Patter." Of the 1,908 articles, Mr. Bennett was able to identify 1,718, or ninety per cent, either as articles the *Digest* actually reprinted or as articles the *Digest* actually produced itself. Mr. Bennett was unable to get scientific data on the other ten per cent because of unanswered letters, unanswered telephones, slammed doors, and blank memories. Of the 1,718 identifiable articles, 720 were merely reprinted, in the old-fashioned meaning of the word, by the *Digest* from other periodicals. Bennett calls these genuine reprints. An additional 316 articles were written solely for the *Digest* and printed there only. Bennett calls these bona-fide originals. The remaining 682 articles were written for the *Digest,* planted in other periodicals, and then "reprinted" by the *Digest.* Bennett calls these plants, or disguised originals. In other figures, 720 articles, or forty-two per cent, were genuine reprints, and 998, or fifty-eight per cent, were either bona-fide or disguised originals. Later samplings made by Bennett show about the same percentages for 1944 and 1945. Thus, approximately three out of every five *Digest* articles now originate in the *Digest's* offices. Or, in fewer words, considerably less than half of its content is reaped from other periodicals. Or, in still fewer words, *The Reader's Digest* is no longer primarily a digest.

This entertaining state of affairs is not so obvious to ordinary magazine-readers, because the *Digest's* planting operations are so scattered. In the five years from 1939 through 1943, the *Digest* planted articles in more than sixty publications. During this period, the *American Mercury* was credited as being its largest source of reprinted articles. Of the seventy-four pieces taken from the *Mercury*, the majority were planted by the *Digest*. More than half the articles credited to the *Rotarian, Hygeia*, the *Kiwanis Magazine, Survey Graphic*, and the *American Legion Magazine* were also originated by the *Digest*. Of forty-seven articles reprinted from *Harper's*, eight were *Digest* plants; of thirty-nine furnished by the *Atlantic Monthly*, eight were plants; of four credited to the *Yale Review*, three are known to be plants; of eight taken from the *Nation*, five were plants; of twenty-six credited to the *New Republic*, eight were plants and thirteen others were on the *Digest's* presses before the *New Republic* appeared on the stands with them. This is a plain indication that they were prepared under what a *New Republic* official has called "a special arrangement." Two, and perhaps more, of the four articles cred-

ited to the *North American Review* were placed
there by the *Digest,* and of four winnowed from
Asia, two were planted. The *Digest* gave *Commonweal* credit for nine reprinted articles; all were
plants. In the same period, twenty-one articles
were credited to the Baltimore *Sunday Sun;* all
were plants. During these five years, the *Digest*
reprinted one or more articles from *Harper's
Bazaar, Free World, Saturday Night, Parents'
Magazine, Woman's Press, National Safety News,
Stage, Yankee, Progressive Education, South Atlantic Quarterly, Family Circle Magazine,* and the
Virginia Quarterly Review; all were plants.

Not every magazine and newspaper that has had
relations with the *Digest* has participated in its
planting system. Between 1939 and 1943, there
were six periodicals which, though they took no
articles from the *Digest,* supplied it with two
dozen or more articles apiece. These were *Life,*
the *American Magazine, Collier's,* the *New
Yorker,* the New York *Times,* and *Fortune,* in the
order of the number of articles reprinted. Among
the other non-collaborating periodicals that furnished only genuine reprints, though fewer than
two dozen, were the *Saturday Evening Post,*

Time, Good Housekeeping, McCall's, Newsweek, Woman's Home Companion, and the New York *Herald Tribune.* Recently, the *New Republic,* the *Nation, Free World,* and *Commonweal* have announced that they will be sown no more. Their reasons range from disagreement with the *Digest's* editorial bias to a lack of interest in the kind of article offered. "We just got fed up with printing their buncombe," the editor of one of the reconstructed journals has explained.

The reasons given by editors who support the planting system are varied, too. Probably the most enticing ones are that it is a handy way to get articles and that the articles don't cost anything. Some substantial publications, such as the *Atlantic Monthly* and the Baltimore *Sun,* however, refuse to accept the pieces as charity; when editors of these periodicals take an article submitted by the *Digest,* they pay the author of the piece at their regular rates. The author has, of course, already been paid by the *Digest.* One free-lance writer who wrote an article the *Digest* planted in *Hygeia* was paid $1,200 by the *Digest* and later got a check from *Hygeia* for $18.50. Though they cannot afford to pay as much as the *Digest,* quite a few old-fashioned publications nevertheless prefer to pay something. "To do otherwise," the editor of a venerable monthly magazine has observed, "is, in my judgment, to be a stooge, or less." Many editors are inclined to take the more broad-minded view of the planting system, however. They like it because it provides them with articles, occasionally by well-known writers; because it gets the name of their magazine before the millions of *Digest* readers; and because, of course, the complete giant-combination editorial offer doesn't cost them a penny. "Look," the editor of a modest periodical that has accepted many *Digest* plants once said, "if you were walking down the street and saw a man giving away twenty-dollar bills, would you walk up and spit in his eye?"

The Reader's Digest feels that its planting operations are completely misunderstood. For example, it is inaccurate, the *Digest* explains to its critics, to say that a piece it sends to another magazine is a planted article; it should be called a coöperatively planned article. Since the *Digest* believes that it is misunderstood, it seems only fair to present the publication's position, and perhaps such a presentation can best be accomplished by adopting the "Mr. Pro and Mr. Con" running-debate technique that the *Digest* itself has often used in dealing with such controversial questions as "Should Post-Mortem Examinations Become Common Procedure?" That form will be followed here in considering the question "Is It Is or Is It Ain't a Digest?" All the statements made by Mr. Pro are quoted verbatim from a report submitted by *The Reader's Digest* to the Board of Education of Passaic, New Jersey, which had expressed to the management of the *Digest* an interest in certain aspects of its procedure, including the operation of the planting system. Mr. Pro's remarks can therefore be assumed to represent the official *Digest* view. He begins:

Mr. Pro: The next charge leveled against the *Digest* had to do with the practice of "planting articles in other magazines." Here the critics of the *Digest* took a very simple routine process in the production of the magazine and distorted it, misrepresented it, and unblushingly lied about it, with the result that there is created in the mind of the uninformed the image of a conspiracy—

Mr. Con: Get to the point, Mr. Pro.

Mr. Pro: Let us look at the facts. It is true that the *Digest* does not confine itself to publishing articles and stories previously and independently published by other magazines. In large part it does just that.

Mr. Con: On the contrary, it does just the opposite, if by "in large part" you mean a major portion—which, I grant you, you wouldn't necessarily have to mean. Over half the articles published in the *Digest* in a five-year period studied by George W. Bennett were not previously and independently published by other magazines. They originated in the office of the *Digest*.

Mr. Pro: But it also published original articles which have appeared nowhere else and it furthermore obtains material which it offers to other magazines prior to publication in the *Digest*. In none of these procedures is there anything secret or sinister.

Mr. Con: Would you mind, then, stating just how many original articles the *Digest* prints and how many it plants, or, as you say, offers to other magazines before publication in the *Digest?*

Mr. Pro: (*No answer.*)

Mr. Con: Proceed.

Mr. Pro: It is true that the *Digest* sometimes offers to other magazines complete articles, condensed versions of which subsequently appear in the *Digest*. Often these articles are worked out in collaboration with the editors of other magazines.

Mr. Con: And more often they are not. As a rule, the editor of a magazine has never seen or heard of a *Digest* plant before it turns up in his office. If the articles were, as you say, worked out in collaboration with the editors of other magazines, how do you explain the fact that editors reject so many of these pieces? The rate of return of articles sent out for planting is, as you know, high. Many editors remark with pride that for every *Digest* plant they accept, they reject from two to four more. But go ahead.

Mr. Pro: A fee is paid to various publications which guarantees to the *Digest* the right to republish their available material. This is simple business practice, and in no sense implies any editorial control of these publications. The core of criticisms of this procedure consists in the accusation that articles politically slanted are farmed out in this way. The balance of facts is all on the other side. How much does *The Reader's Digest* influence the policies of other publications on political or economic matters? Or how much—

MR. CON: Sorry to interrupt, Mr. Pro, but you're getting off the subject again. What you were going to say is that only a small percentage of *Digest* plants are concerned with such controversial issues as economics, government, politics, and industrial and international relations. That may well be, but perhaps the reason is that not all other magazines want to be sown with *Digest* articles concerned with these issues, or with your point of view on them. Can you think, offhand, for example, of a half-dozen magazines that would have been glad to take the responsibility for printing that curious *Digest* piece called "Our Deep Dark Secrets in Latin America"? Many people, you recall, considered the article so mischievous and full of misinformation that they agreed with Senator Joseph Guffey, who said in Congress that the *Digest* owed an apology and an explanation to the people of the United States for publishing it. Anyway, the question isn't how many articles on controversial topics the *Digest* plants. The question is how many articles on *all* topics it plants.

The fact that it plants so many is the real core of the criticisms.

MR. PRO (*Serenely*): Certainly there is no reason to attribute any possible "influencing of other editors, or periodicals, or public opinion itself" to the practice of offering an article on the habits of animals to a nature magazine, or a report on dental progress to a dentists' journal. This is not a public disservice but a public service.

MR. CON: Oh, come now, Mr. Pro. You're talking as if *The Reader's Digest* were the Rockefeller Foundation. The *Digest* is a commercial enterprise, like any other magazine, not a philanthropy. It gives planted articles to nature magazines and dentists' journals and other publications so it can use the names of these periodicals on its cover and over the articles and thus keep up the pretense that it is a reprint magazine. If it isn't solely for this reason that the *Digest* plants these pieces, why does it go to all the trouble of planting them? Why doesn't the *Digest* simply print them as original articles? Furthermore, Mr. Pro, you refer to the planting business as "a very simple routine process," giving the impression that it is common practice in the trade. Of course it isn't. The planting system is unique with the *Digest,* and it doesn't seem so very routine even to the *Digest.* For one thing, the job takes the full time of a senior editor of the *Digest,* Mr. Howard Florance, and his staff, who are kept busy peddling these so-called "coöperatively planned" articles. And don't forget that time the *Digest* condensed an article from the *Nation* so ingeniously that it ran four hundred and sixty-eight words longer than the article it was condensed from. Apparently the *Digest* occasionally neglects to get the coöperation of other editors very far in advance. Many letters accompanying articles sent out for planting are dated only two or three days before the *Digest* goes to press. "We are hoping," one of these letters reads, as you may recall, "to print the story in our July *Reader's Digest,* out about June twenty-fifth, and would be happy to credit it to your periodical." The letter is dated May 21st, one day after the normal date for closing your July issue. Other letters give the impression of even greater hurry. "If you don't want it," one reads, "will you let us know promptly? Or, rather, will you forgive me if I call up Monday afternoon to ask if you are at all interested?" Another:

"Would you be very kind and read it as soon as possible, as we are making up the next issue? Perhaps you would be able to telephone some time today?" Some have a pleading note. One, scribbled in pencil, says, "Can you use this? Before Jan. 25. In haste." In haste indeed. The letter was written two days after the usual *Digest* press time.

Since the rate of rejections is high, Mr. Pro, many articles have to be peddled from one magazine office to another before they are finally planted. Even then, trouble sometimes occurs. For example, there was an article about a South American newspaper that the *Digest* planted, or thought it had planted, in a periodical that I will call *Good Neighbor*. In checking the piece, the editors of *Good Neighbor* discovered some errors, decided not to print it after all, and notified the *Digest*. But the *Digest* had already gone to press with the article, confidently crediting *Good Neighbor* as the source. So the *Digest* appeared with the article which it said it had "Condensed from *Good Neighbor*." This was a rare feat; the article from which the condensation was presumably made had never been published by any periodical on earth.

No, planting articles is not very simple, Mr. Pro.

It is a tricky business. Do you remember a magazine called the *Living Age?* It was, as you know, once an old and respected periodical, but it fell on hard times and was bought for fifteen thousand dollars in June, 1938, by three men, Joseph Hilton Smyth, Walter Grey Matheson, and Irvine Harvey Williams. The money to buy the magazine was furnished by the Japanese government through the local Japanese vice-consul, Sintaro Fukushima, who also helped underwrite the magazine's overhead by contributing about twenty-five hundred dollars a month. In September of 1942, Smyth and his colleagues were arrested by the F.B.I. and later pleaded guilty to having run the *Living Age* in behalf of the Japanese government between June, 1938, and December, 1941. During this time they had accepted approximately a hundred and fifty thousand dollars from the Japs. Smyth and his colleagues were sentenced to seven years in a federal penitentiary. While the *Living Age* was being run for the benefit of the Japanese, the *Digest* reprinted thirteen articles from it. Actually, the majority were plants, or, to use the *Digest's* phrase, articles coöperatively planned by the editors of the *Digest* and the editors of the

Living Age. Three of the pieces were written by *Digest* editors. Of all the articles furnished by the *Digest,* possibly the one that caused Sintaro Fukushima the most amusement was the piece the *Digest* planted in the May, 1940, issue of the *Living Age* and "reprinted" in the *Digest* in June. This was entitled "How Smart Are the Japanese?" Of course, the editors of the *Digest* had no way of knowing that the *Living Age* was a Japanese propaganda organ, so there was nothing treasonable about dealing with it. But the case does illustrate that planting is not at all a routine procedure. It is an involved technique, and sometimes even perilous. Since you said earlier, Mr. Pro, that there is nothing secret about the planting system, do you feel that to describe its operation constitutes what the *Digest* has called a smear?

MR. PRO: In view of these facts, it clearly appears that the so-called "planting" of articles has to deal with a variety of subjects, very few of which are controversial in character; that, in fact, what is a simple magazine procedure has been misrepresented and made into a smear. It has been alleged that the *Digest* has changed. In a sense

this is true. . . . The *Digest* has outgrown the limitations of selecting its material from magazines
alone, and now includes selections from newspapers, books, and professional and trade journals; from public speeches, from radio programs,
motion-picture scripts, and from any other source,
including any original source, that provides material which, in the judgment of its editors, will be
of interest to its readers. . . . So the *Digest* re-
mains the true digest of American literature
today.

MR. CON: *Caveat emptor.*

4

CHAPPAQUA, U. S. A.

A VISIT to *The Reader's Digest,* like a visit to the Soviet Union, is bound to be a rewarding experience, for each in its way is powerful, perplexing, and but dimly understood. The value of going to Russia has been amply demonstrated by Mr. W. L. White, publisher of the Emporia *Gazette* and one of the eighteen Roving Editors of *The Reader's Digest.* In the spring of 1944, Mr. White accompanied Mr. Eric Johnston, then president of the United States Chamber of Commerce, on a five-week visit to the Soviet Union. On his return, Mr. White wrote the book called "Report on the Russians," a condensation of which was published in *The Reader's Digest.* During his travels in the Soviet Union, Mr. White passed out invitations to various Russians to visit the United States, and it so happened—or at least one might imagine it so happened—that one of these, Mr. White's Soviet counterpart, Nikolai Popkov, one of the innumerable Gadding Editors of the Russian digest magazine *Minimag,* decided to make the trip. Mr. Popkov, a single-minded fellow, came over and spent his entire stay—a day—in and around *The Reader's Digest,* so that he could learn all about the world's most popular magazine. Popkov took nothing for granted. A man from Soviet Russia is like a man from Mars; he looks around him and says, "My, my!" On his return to Russia, Popkov wrote a book about his trip, a condensation of which appeared beforehand in *Minimag*. A condensation of that condensation, which unfortunately may have suffered somewhat in translation, is printed below:

I begin my visit to *The Reader's Digest*. I go to Grand Central Station early in the morning and buy a ticket to Chappaqua, New York, where the *Digest* factory is situated. At the railroad station in Chappaqua, I am met by a delegation of *Digest* editors. When my good friend Mr. White visited Russia, he complained a good deal about how shabby and underfed my countrymen looked, so I am naturally inclined to make a few similar observations about these editors. In honesty, I must report that all of them look as though they've just had a good meal. They do not look shabby, either, but I am not very favorably impressed by their clothes. Their coats do not match their pants. I was to learn later that this is not because the editors cannot afford to buy a whole suit at one time but because they prefer to wear what they call the sports jacket and slacks. This seems to be the more or less standard uniform for *Digest* editors.

My hosts bundle me into a car and we start for the *Digest* factory, which is in the country, two or three miles from town. On the way, I exchange a few words with the Executive Editor, Kenneth W. Payne, a thin, wiry, taut-looking man of fifty-five who has worked for the *Digest* since 1931. In the old days, Payne tells me, the *Digest* had its offices on the upper floors of two bank buildings in the neighboring town of Pleasantville. As the magazine grew, more space was needed, so in 1939 De-Witt Wallace, the owner and editor of the *Digest*, built the present plant. Since then, a wing has been added, and the entire factory is now valued at five million rubles, or about a million dollars.

We turn off the highway onto a private road, and presently I get my first view of the *Digest* plant. I am not too fond of the architecture, but as I often say—and I am sure my good friend Mr. White, who was not much impressed by Soviet architecture, would agree with me—*"De gustibus non est disputandum."* I am told that the *Digest* factory was inspired by a building in Williamsburg, Virginia, which appealed to both Editor Wallace and his wife. The building is a three-story red-brick Georgian structure, from the center of which rises an enormous white cupola. It is surrounded by wide lawns and wooded hills. Everything about it looks tidy and peaceful.

Executive Editor Payne takes me on a quick tour of the building. The interior was decorated under the supervision of Editor Wallace's wife, and Payne tells me that most visitors say the furnishings are tasteful and luxurious. The editors' offices are on the ground floor, and the circulation, promotion, and other business departments on the upper two. Editor Wallace's office, a large room in the southwest corner of the first floor, has a fire-

place, with a davenport on either side, as well as a
large desk, comfortable chairs, occasional tables,
built-in bookshelves, deep-piled green carpet, and
Venetian blinds. On the desk, mantelpiece, and
tables are several carved jade figures. The offices
of the subordinate editors are furnished somewhat less lavishly, but all are soundproofed and
done in pleasing pastels. Some have paintings on
the walls and bowls of cut flowers on the desks.
Also on the first floor is an octagonally shaped
library, paneled in fine wood, for the use of the
editors. In the library I find that a small banquet
has been spread for me. This does not surprise me,
as we Russians go in for this sort of thing a good
deal ourselves. It sometimes happens that our
guests, like my good friend Mr. White, do not care
much for the kind of food we have to offer, which
consists mainly of champagne and caviar, and get
to complaining about the fare. But as I often say,
"De gustibus." Personally, I like champagne and
caviar, so I am a little disappointed to find that the
food for this banquet in my honor consists of
peanut-butter sandwiches. It seems that Editor
Wallace is convinced that peanut butter is loaded
with health-giving properties. At one time he had

such sandwiches distributed daily to all his employees, until he discovered that some of the workers were hiding the refreshments in their desk drawers. I try to choke down a couple of sandwiches, but I find them very dry, so I ask Payne for a bottle of champagne to help them along. He leaves the room and returns with a glass of ice water. He explains that there is no champagne on the premises. Nor is there any caviar.

So that I can see the rest of the factory, Payne turns me over to Office Manager H. G. Wilcox, a debonair young man who gets things done and has a habit of snapping his fingers to indicate that everything is under control. Following Wilcox, I waltz around the business departments to the strains of "The Blue Danube," which happens to be the number coming out of the loudspeakers there. Orchestral music is played for the workers at intervals during the day, an idea thought up by Editor Wallace, who believes that music has therapeutic value. I notice that most of the workers here are women, as is the case in factories back home. I stop and engage one of the workers, a young woman running a stenciling machine, in conversation. While Wilcox hangs around snapping his fingers, I ask the young woman about working conditions at the *Digest*.

"Well," she says, "we work five days a week, from eight-thirty in the morning to three-thirty in the afternoon. When we finish in the afternoon, we are serenaded over the loudspeakers with 'Good Night, Ladies.' We have thirty minutes for lunch and two ten-minute recess periods, one in the morning and one in the afternoon. We spend our recesses in one of the fourteen lounges, which were decorated in chintzes by Mrs. Wallace and are scattered around the building, and we eat our lunch in the company cafeteria, which serves a nice meal for twenty-five cents. Once a month, we have a long week end lasting from Thursday afternoon to Monday morning, and we get three weeks' vacation each year with pay. The minimum wage here is seventy-five dollars a month, but everybody also gets an annual bonus amounting to at least two months' salary. After we've been here a certain length of time, we can qualify for the retirement plan. Besides all this, we have an infirmary right here in the building, where, upon being hired, everybody, including editors, receives a complete medical examination, from a Wasser-

mann test to a fluoroscope examination for tuberculosis, free. At Christmastime, we all get together
and sing carols and Mrs. Wallace sends each of us
girls a dozen long-stemmed roses. Once Editor
Wallace took all the workers to New York City for
a nice dinner at a fancy hotel and then to the
theater. What more could a girl ask?" I think of
two or three things, but I can see that this is no
time for dialectics.

I rejoin Wilcox and we go back to the library,
where I find that another banquet has been prepared for me. Same sandwiches. No champagne.
No caviar, salted or unsalted. The purpose of this
affair is to introduce me to the editorial staff,
which numbers about one hundred and twenty-five
people. Dozens of guests are milling around, and I
ask one of them how many of those present are
editors. "Oh, we're practically all editors here,"
the man says happily, adding that besides Editor
Wallace and his wife, the *Digest* has an Executive
Editor, a Managing Editor, eleven Senior Editors,
eighteen Roving Editors, and twenty Associate
Editors, making a total of fifty-three. I ask how
many articles are published in a typical issue of
the *Digest* and learn that there are about thirty. I

quickly figure out that the *Digest* has almost twice as many editors as it has articles per issue. Or, in other words, if the work at the *Digest* were distributed equally among all the editors, each editor would be responsible for approximately one-half of one article a month. My good friend Mr. White had quite a few things to say about Soviet inefficiency. Hmm. [Translator's note: What Popkov actually said was *"Ekh, i takoi molodetz eshcho smeyet rassuzhdat o poryadkakh na proisvodstve,"* for which there is no English equivalent.]

I see the Soviet's old friend Max Eastman in the group and am about to rush over to embrace him, but I check myself. Max is no longer one of us. He is a Roving Editor now and he has changed his mind about private property. I understand he owns quite a bit of it. Too bad about Max.

I eat another peanut-butter sandwich, talk with many of the editors, and rapidly arrive at several conclusions.

Generally speaking, *Digest* editors are middle-aged, from the middle class, with middle-sized talents. Like Editor Wallace, who is the son of a Doctor of Divinity, the grandson of a minister, the son-in-law of a minister, and the brother-in-law of two ministers, several *Digest* editors have clerical backgrounds. The average age of the dozen or so top *Digest* editors is a bit beyond the half-century mark. The more formidable names on the magazine's masthead—J. P. McEvoy, William Hard, Max Eastman, Paul de Kruif—belong to men of the last generation. The salaries paid to *Digest* editors are, even by American standards, enough to make your head swim. Editor Wallace pays himself $99,500 a year, and, since he owns a little over half of the *Digest's* stock, his income—before, as capitalist writers put it, taxes—is around a quarter of a million dollars. Mrs. Wallace, who owns a little under half of the stock, has a comfortable income, too. Executive Editor Payne is paid $84,500 a year. The incomes of the other subordinate editors are also impressive. Senior Editors are paid in the neighborhood of $50,000, Roving Editors $30,000, and Associate Editors $15,000. The editors, like the workers, are paid partly in salary and partly in bonus. Payne, for example, receives $48,000 as salary and $36,500 as bonus. The bonus system provides an incentive to the editors to conduct themselves with decorum for a full year.

Most *Digest* editors attended college, are married, and have middle-sized families. Except for the Roving Editors, who do not have offices in the *Digest* building, nearly all *Digest* editors live in comfortable country homes in the vicinity of the factory, send their children to the same schools, belong to the same country club, and share an existence as patterned as that of the workers on a collective farm. Unlike collective farmers, *Digest* editors are not bound to their jobs by national law. They are bound, however, by the economic law of increasing returns, which has as its corollary the law of diminishing independence. The longer editors stay at the *Digest,* the more money they make, and the more they make, the more they spend, and eventually they are making so much money that they can't afford to work anywhere else. Nothing like this can befall a Russian.

Since Editor Wallace is the power from whom all financial blessings flow, his hired hands vie with each other in their aim to please, and as a result there is enough intrigue at the *Digest* to merit the passing interest of a de' Medici. Editors seldom openly oppose Wallace on any matter, major or minor, and they try to remember him appropriately at Christmas. This is not an easy thing to do. What can you give a man from whom you have every reason to expect a bonus running into five or six figures? [Translator's note: Popkov was thinking in rubles, of course; in dollars, the bonuses would run into only four or five figures.] Perhaps the most original solution of this problem was made some years ago by one of the *Digest* editors, Henry Morton Robinson. He saved all the memoranda he received from Wallace, along with carbons of his own replies, and had them put together in a book, handsomely bound in fine leather, to make a Christmas gift. Some of the memoranda, I understand, are very interesting; e. g., "Dear Robbie: Thanks for triple-spacing that manuscript. Makes it easier to read."

It is now time for me to have lunch with the Senior Editors. I expect to eat in the *Digest's* cafeteria, but I discover that the executives here do not eat with the workers. *Digest* executives have private dining rooms, expensively furnished and equipped with silver service and fine china. I suppose this is all right, but throughout our lunch

I cannot help thinking of the workers down there in the cafeteria. I hope they are getting enough to eat.

My host at lunch is the No. 2 man of the *Digest,* General Manager Albert L. Cole. Cole, who is hardheaded, politically astute, and forceful, has great influence with Wallace, and gets credit for much of the *Digest's* enormous expansion in recent years. Before going to work as the *Digest's* chief business official, Cole had a similar job with *Popular Science.* One of his responsibilities is circulation, which has doubled since his arrival, in 1939. In addition, Cole often acts as the official company spokesman, is the magazine's chief trouble shooter and apologist, and is Wallace's alter ego in the handling of many other management burdens.

Being a journalist, I am less interested in Cole than in the Senior Editors, and, as the food is a trifle slow in arriving, I have ample time to size them up before we begin to eat. (I might point out that there is no caviar, pressed or unpressed.) The two Seniors who impress me most, for varying reasons, are Ralph E. Henderson and Paul Palmer. In many ways, Henderson represents the

Digest before, and Palmer the *Digest* after, the Revolution. The *Digest* Revolution occurred in the middle thirties. Before the Revolution, the *Digest* was solely a reprint magazine. After the Revolution, it became a magazine containing a preponderance of original articles. Before the Revolution, the *Digest* was a small business, with a small staff of editors whose backgrounds were more ecclesiastical than journalistic. After the Revolution, the *Digest* became a big business and acquired a large staff. The new editors were professionals and worldly. Before the Revolution, the *Digest* was more or less neutral on most political and economic matters. After the Revolution, the *Digest* left the middle of the road and took a sharp turn to the Right. I cannot say that this pleases me.

Henderson had almost perfect qualifications for a pre-Revolution editor. He was born in the jungles of Burma, the son of missionaries, and, after coming to this country to go to Harvard, went back to the jungle, where he taught for four years in missionary schools. Returning to the United States in 1925, he met the Wallaces, who were then putting out their little magazine by themselves. He was hired as business manager, a job that was the favorite proving ground for *Digest* editors in the early days. Two years later he became an Associate Editor, when an ex-preacher named Harold A. Lynch was hired to fill the business post, and in 1940, Henderson was advanced to the rank of Senior Editor. Henderson is tall, boyish-looking, earnest, and, at least by *Digest* standards, liberal in outlook. Since the middle of 1945, he has had the unofficial title of New York "contact man," which means that he has offices in the Chrysler Building in New York City. His assignment is to deal with writers and literary agents, look for new talent, and act as Wallace's ambassador in the country's journalistic capital.

Except for the fact that he is also a Harvard man, Paul Palmer differs rather markedly from Henderson. Palmer is a handsome man and a fastidious dresser, polished and sophisticated, and was once described by an acquaintance as "plausible." He has been described by Editor Wallace as "a good old-line American." He has described himself as a "medievalist," by which, he explains, he means that he has a fancy for the colorful Middle Ages. "Is there anything wrong," he has disarmingly inquired of some of his *Digest* associates, "in being a medievalist?" Palmer was a *Digest* man off and on for a couple of years before 1942, and since then he has been a Senior Editor. His function has never been altogether clear to all of his colleagues, but his influence with Wallace, I am told, is tremendous, a situation that may be traced to the fact that Palmer is definite, realistic, and, by comparison with other *Digest* editors, independent. Wallace may find it refreshing to employ an editor who can say no.

Palmer has had wide experience as a journalist. After Harvard, he became a reporter on the Baltimore *Sun*, then went to work for the St. Louis *Post-Dispatch*, and later became Sunday editor of the New York *World*. From 1935 until 1939, when he went over to the *Digest*, he was owner and editor of the *American Mercury*. While he was on the *Mercury*, he printed several pieces by Harold Lord Varney, an exceedingly conservative author, and a dozen articles by Lawrence Dennis, whom *Life* once described as "America's No. 1 Fascist author" and one of the "two prize examples of native American Fascism." Dennis is the author of a book called *The Coming American Fascism*, and was one of the thirty defendants in the recent American mass sedition trial that was interrupted by the death of the presiding judge. When Palmer came to the *Digest,* he called Dennis in as a paid consultant. "We were entitled to play along with Dennis," Wallace later explained to Kenneth Stewart, a writer for *PM,* "until we were sure that he would be of no use to us. After all, he was a recognized economist for a Wall Street firm, and Palmer offered him a nominal sum to help in a critical way, making suggestions. We didn't get a nickel's worth of value out of him." I can say that this pleases me.

During the early afternoon, I inspect the production line to learn how *Digest* articles are manufactured. The factory turns out two models of articles—reprints and originals. The output is roughly divided on a sixty-forty basis, with the originals in the majority. The assembly line for reprints, which I examine hurriedly, is similar to that used in many factories, except that at the *Digest* it runs in reverse. Instead of putting things together, it takes things apart. In a Marxian sense, this is not "production."

The *Digest* subscribes to two hundred general

magazines and three hundred specialized journals. The first readers study the first group carefully and glance through the second, grading the articles according to a system like the one used for grading papers in school. Of the dozens of articles given high grades each month by the first readers, sixty or seventy are chosen by the Associate Editors for further consideration, and tentative condensations of these are made. There is no prescribed percentage of cutting for an article, but the general idea is to get rid of as much wordage as possible. As a rule, a condensed article at this stage has been brought down to about a quarter of the length of the original. Some pieces, especially those containing a preponderance of ideas rather than facts, cannot stand the strain of such surgery and die on the editors' tables. Out of the sixty or seventy articles that undergo the condensing operation, fifty may survive for the consideration of the top editors. Again, many are culled but few are chosen. Usually, a dozen articles survive this winnowing, and these are given a second editing. Editor Wallace does some of this final precision work himself. He is a perfectionist, by his own acknowledgment, and he frequently keeps snipping at a piece right up to press time.

In the excising process, adjectives and adverbs are the first casualties. Descriptive and stylistic words and phrases are next killed. Out of a paragraph of exposition leading up to a one-sentence conclusion, perhaps only the conclusion will be left. Qualifying phrases are snuffed out. There is often some rearrangement of material, and here and there a connective is added. In the course of the operation, the emphasis of the article may shift perceptibly, but as a rule the viewpoint is left intact; rather than make an elaborate effort to alter the viewpoint of an article to coincide with theirs, the *Digest* editors simply pass the piece by. If literature can be condensed like milk, a premise, if *Minimag* will forgive me, with which a considerable body of opinion does not agree, the *Digest* has the most expert technical facility for doing it. However, the magazine's enthusiasm for its condensing process seems extravagant. Each article, the *Digest* once announced, is "condensed so brilliantly that not an essential idea is lost. Even the characteristic flavor of the original is retained. IT IS the original, in concentrated, time-saving form.'' This may be true, in the sense that a skeleton is the original party in concentrated form, but with a little meat on him he might be more fun to have around the house.

Since I have seen the factory, I now think I ought to see the finished product. I tell one of the editors that I would like to examine some *Digest* articles as they have appeared in print, so he ushers me into the library and gives me several bound volumes of the magazine to look at. I look through them and quickly come to several conclusions.

In the first place, the most remarkable thing about *Digest* articles is their titles. They are so uniformly staggering that, as one reader said in a letter the *Digest* printed, ''it's hard to choose among them.'' That reader said he solved the problem by studying the list of articles on the cover and then reading first the pieces which, judging by their titles, ''would seem likely to beguile me least.'' This appears to be a sound idea, so I use the same system in making a list of the articles I intend to read, and in the course of doing this I discover that they fall into clear-cut categories.

Digest titles are of four general types. First, in accordance with this reverse grading system, is the Ecclesiastical, which includes such beguiling samples as "Harvesting the Lord's Acre," "The Lord's Tiny Poultry," "A Businessman Looks at Prayer," "The Home That Prayer Built," and "Does Anything Come After Death?" The second is the Personal type: "I Have Four Parents," "I Like Skunks," "I Saw a Commando Cry," "I Ran Away with My Wife," "I Would Not Divorce Him Now," and "I Sent My Father to an Old Men's Home." Sometimes types one and two are combined with such results as "I Was an Atheist Until . . . ," "I Am on a Church Strike!," "I'm Going Back to Church," "I Believe in Immortality." As for me, I'm not a churchgoer.

The third, or Comical, type of title usually contains a pun. For example, an article about justices of the peace was cleverly called "Justice by the Piece," and another about a town in Texas named Howe was humorously titled "Here's Howe." The wittiest title of all, I think—although, because of language difficulties, I distrust my own judgment

—was the one attached to an article about a cow named Elsie that is alluded to frequently in the advertisements of a milk company named Borden. This was called "Elsie, the Beautiful Lactress." I am sorry that in Russia we have no advertising of this type.

The fourth, or Sensational, type of title is the one the *Digest* uses most often. This type has an electrifying effect on the reader and practically forces him to sit right down and read the article. Some examples are: "Our Enemy, the Fly," "Survive at Sea by Eating and Drinking Fish!," "My First Funeral," "New Hope for Cross-Eyes," "Must You Keep Your Heart in Cold Storage?," "From Garbage to Good Government," "Detroit's Fighting Milkman," "Are You Neglecting the Wonder Bean?," and "America's Debt to the Hen."

I pick out a number of articles in this fourth category, which I consider the least beguiling, and start to read, but I find myself reading a bit of one article and then skipping to the next, reading a little of that, and then going on to another. I can't seem to get interested. The trouble, I finally discover, lies in the leads. I suppose I ought to explain that we journalists use the term "lead" to describe the opening sentences or paragraphs of an article. Usually, a writer tries to make the lead compelling enough to get and hold the reader's attention, but I'm not sure that writers published in the *Digest* are consistent about this. I start one article which begins:

> Hi, girls! Remember me? That man who sticks his neck out every so often to put you right about your clothes and hats so you can contrive to attract us? I'm back again with a complaint.

I stop right there and try another:

> The spontaneous revival of old-fashioned square dancing is a national phenomenon.

And another:

> Three neighbors of mine in suburban New York asked to feed molasses to my cow. Flossie liked the fare and thrived. Because she did, she in her bovine way helped to feed molasses to two million southwestern cattle this year.

Then another:

> A bank used to be an imposing institution sheathed in icy austerity; today it is a service station, eager to meet the humblest of financial needs.

And still another:

> I once had a rather memorable experience with a waterlily.

And then:

> Automobile driver, know thyself! My friend Schwartz didn't.

Before I have a chance to sample any more articles, I am interrupted by a couple of men who come into the library and introduce themselves. I don't quite get the names, but they sound something like Mr. Tex Jones and Mr. Rex Brown. They say they have been selling free-lance articles to the *Digest* for several years. They have appointments to see one of the editors about some pieces. I ask how they like working for the *Digest*.

"It's a living," says Tex.

"You mean," says Rex, "it's a living when you finally get paid."

"That's right," Tex says. "The complaint we free-lance writers have is that it takes these editors forever to make up their minds. You submit a piece and then you wait around for weeks, maybe months, before you know whether it's going to be accepted or rejected. I guess the trouble is that all the editors have the authority to reject a piece, but only Wally—that's Editor Wallace—has the authority to accept one."

"Wally's all right," Rex says. "You can get along fine when you work directly with him."

"Sure," says Tex, "but when Wally's away, these other editors play hell with a piece. Like that one I sold them a few months ago. I talked the idea for that over with Wally; he liked it and told me to go ahead and write it. I did and sent it up. Six weeks go by and no word. Finally I call up and talk to one of the Seniors, and he says Wally's out of town, but he'll read the piece himself and let me know. Three weeks later, I get the piece back with a note from this Senior saying sorry, but he's afraid they can't use it. I called him up and raised the roof. 'For God's sake,' I said, 'Wally ordered that piece himself, and I think the least you can do is to let him see it.' The Senior was reluctant to promise this, but finally he said he would. As soon as Wally read it, he bought it, and gave me a bonus besides. Rex, tell the man what the editor of that big ladies' magazine said about these subordinate editors.''

''Oh,'' says Rex, ''he thinks they all act like a bunch of amateurs. 'But the *Digest* has got so much money,' this editor said, 'that they don't have to be smart.' The statement is a little illogical, but you get the idea.''

''That reminds me,'' Tex says, ''of what Alec Woollcott once said to a friend at the Players. 'The *Digest*,' Alec said, 'not only destroys the pleasure of writing but of reading.' ''

''If there's so much trouble about working for the *Digest*,'' I say, ''why do you go on working for them?''

''Because of a little thing called money,'' Rex says.

''The *Digest* has plenty, and they don't mind handing it out,'' Tex says. ''The minimum pay for an article is a thousand dollars, and regulars like Rex and me, who do quite a few pieces, get twice that much. In addition, we can count on a bonus of a few hundred dollars every so often.''

"You get mad as hell at their amateurishness," Rex says, "but then, out of the blue, Wally sends you half a grand for some reason or another and it sort of soothes you. For example, I ran across what I thought was a good article in an old issue of a magazine. The *Digest* had never reprinted it, so I dropped Wally a note and told him about it. I got a note back from Wally saying he'd print it and thanking me for my coöperation, and along with it a check for five hundred skins. They're good about expense accounts, too. Nobody around here worries about money."

"No, sir," says Tex. "One of the Seniors once said to me, 'Our biggest problem is what to do with all our money.' "

"Maybe that's part of the trouble," Rex says. "Maybe the money does something to the subordinate editors. They want to rewrite everything they get their hands on."

"Anyway," says Tex, "it takes them a month to rewrite an article that a good editor could fix with a pencil in half an hour. They're rewrite-happy."

"But if you think they're hard on our stuff," Rex says, "you ought to see what they do to unsolicited manuscripts they sometimes buy. Tell him about that birth-control article, Tex.''

''That was an article,'' Tex says, ''called 'A Catholic Mother Looks at Planned Parenthood,' and it was signed Frances Jameson. That was a pseudonym. The author's a friend of mine, and she wrote me about her experience. Mrs. Jameson, as I'll call her, read an article in the *Digest* that was favorable to birth control. She is a Catholic and had done some writing, so she wrote an article presenting her personal Catholic viewpoint and sent it to the *Digest*. After a while, she got a letter from the *Digest* saying they were interested in the piece but that they were turning it over to one of their Catholic editors, who would, as they said, 'endeavor to strengthen it a bit.' Eventually, Mrs. Jameson received a telegram from the *Digest* telling her the piece had been accepted and a proof of the revised version was being mailed to her. She was so pleased she told all her friends and even sent Wally a telegram telling him how proud and elated she was. Her elation was dampened when she received the revised version. Here, I think I've got her letter in my pocket. She says, 'Except for the title and a couple of paragraphs, it wasn't my article at all, and it seemed to me that the entire tone of the thing had been changed. This was probably the *official* Catholic viewpoint much more than my own, and no doubt that was what they wanted to give. I felt strongly, however, that my own very personal, undogmatic article would help the Catholic cause a lot more than theirs, and after being swamped with so-called fan mail, I'm doubly sure of it.' "

"Just a minute," I say. "If Mrs. Jameson was so disappointed, why didn't she get together with the editors and straighten matters out, or simply refuse to let them print it?"

"You forget that little matter of money," says Tex. "In the same envelope with the proof was a check for something over a grand, and Mrs. Jameson happens to be a human being like the rest of us. In the second place, there was no time to straighten anything out. She got the proof on the afternoon of the eighteenth of the month. It had been delayed because of insufficient postage. And along with the proof was a letter from the *Digest* explaining that they were going to press with the article on the twentieth. 'We have gone to considerable pains,' the letter said, 'to augment your original with well-documented facts. It is our hope that you will get this [proof] back to us immediately with as few changes as possible.' Now do you see what I mean about amateurishness?"

"Do you mean," I say, "that the *Digest* handles all its original articles this way?"

"I don't know about *all* of them," Tex says. "I suppose a lot of articles go through without so much rewriting or without this kind of rush act, but it's quite a problem. For instance—"

Rex is interrupted by a secretary who comes into the library and tells him that it is time for his appointment.

"So long, Popkov," Rex says. "I got to see a man about some greenbacks."

I look at my watch and see that it is time to leave for the farewell banquet Editor Wallace is giving for me at his home. The Wallace estate, which is called High Winds, is in Mt. Kisco, several miles from the factory. I am whisked there in a limousine driven by a chauffeur in livery. In front of the house, approached along a wide gravel driveway, there is a large field, sufficiently long and flat so that Editor Wallace can use it as an airplane landing field. I am admitted to the house by a Japanese butler, who takes my wraps and says, "Go to rumpus room, prease." Then he disappears, leaving me alone in the foyer. As nearly as I can make out, the style of the foyer is Norman. It has a stone floor that looks something like a cobblestone street in a Norman village, and there is a large fireplace. In front of the fireplace sits a little pair of sabots.

I set out to look for what the butler calls the rumpus room, but as I have no idea where it is, or even what it is, I do quite a bit of aimless wandering about the place. If I were to describe High Winds in a word, I would say it is opulent. I have heard at the factory that Editor Wallace's wife decorated High Winds all by herself, but as I walk from one room to another I find it hard to believe that one person, unassisted, could have combined so many periods, styles, and colors. The living room, which is about forty-five feet long and thirty-five feet wide, is a pousse-café of a room— blue, yellow, green, and baby pink. Like nearly every other room in the house, it has a copy of the current issue of *The Reader's Digest* lying by itself on a table. Beyond the living room is Mrs.

Wallace's writing room, which is hung profusely
with tapestries and has an enormous desk. On top
of the desk are compartments filled with envelopes,
letter paper of various sizes and shapes, and correspondence cards, all of which are engraved
"High Winds." Before I'm through, I learn that
this name is on just about everything, including
the bath towels and, down in the stables, the horse
blankets.

Doing my best to keep out of drafts, I walk
through a number of other rooms. I remember in
particular the breakfast room, done in black and
chromium, with a large picture window, on either
side of which hangs an enormous bird cage filled
with tropical birds. Then there is Mrs. Wallace's
flower room, a circular room containing a complete
line of gardening equipment, bamboo furniture,
and shelves and shelves of vases. The house has a
circular tower, at the top of which is Editor Wallace's study. You get to it by climbing narrow
stairs. This room has a magnificent view. It is
furnished quite simply. In the bookshelves are
beautifully bound volumes of *The Reader's Digest*. One of the bedrooms in the house, by the way,
has what is probably the thickest white fur rug

east of Siberia. And there is one Hollywood-type bathroom. A person reclining in the tub can flip a switch and the ceiling twinkles with stars. I do not think much of this notion. [Translator's note: Popkov's comment, *"Ya dumayu, chto eto pogannaya ideya,"* somehow sounds more petulant in the original.]

I am experimenting with putting up and taking down the stars when the butler comes in, says he has been sent to search for me, and leads me downstairs to the rumpus room. This room is equipped with a pool table, a ping-pong table, and a bar, and opens out onto an Italian garden. The other guests, mostly editors and executives of the *Digest,* have already assembled and are clustered around Editor Wallace, nodding their heads. I expect to be introduced to Wallace, who is a sturdy, good-looking man of fifty-seven, but I cannot fight my way through the editors surrounding him. I look around for Mrs. Wallace and see her standing across the room talking with Office Manager Wilcox. As nobody pays any attention to me, I decide to shoot a game of pool, but I have no more than chalked the cue when Editor Wallace comes over. I say hello and he says hello. Then Mrs. Wallace comes over, plucks her husband's sleeve, and says, "Darling, you're neglecting your other guests." Editor Wallace walks back to his editors. It is possible that Mrs. Wallace has a certain influence with Mr. Wallace. It is also possible that she does not admire the Soviet. After all, she is half-owner of *The Reader's Digest,* which is worth, an idiomatic guest tells me, about fifteen million "smackers."

Soon dinner is announced. I am about to sit down near Editor Wallace when Wilcox steps up, snaps his fingers, and ushers me to a chair some distance away from my host. When everyone is finally seated, I notice, on Wallace's right, Editor Max Eastman, and on his left an elderly, well-dressed gentleman whom I haven't seen anywhere around the factory. I ask a guest seated next to me who the stranger is, and he says he is a very old friend of Wallace's named Pendleton Dudley. I say I should like to know more about Dudley.

"So would I," the guest says, "but like many people in the public-relations business, Dudley doesn't care for publicity about himself. People used to refer to Dudley as Wallace's Harry Hopkins, but I suppose now they would call him Wallace's Jimmy Byrnes. Neither description would please Dudley very much, because describing Dudley's dislike of most things connected with New Dealism as monumental would be understating the case. Dudley is a self-made man who rose from modest beginnings to the place where he can now name such other successful men as Eddie Rickenbacker among his friends. He is head of Pendleton Dudley Associates, a publicity firm whose clients are mainly trade associations, such as the Florida Citrus Commission and the Can Manufacturers Institute. Another of his important accounts is the American Meat Institute, which he founded in 1919 and which now represents fourteen of the leading packers, who handle the major share of the country's meat. Dudley knows big business like the back of his hand. He is what we in this country call a sound businessman. Dudley has known Wallace for over twenty years—ever since Wallace rented quarters over the garage on Dudley's estate in Pleasantville back in the *Digest's* early days. They have remained close friends. For example, Dudley is one of the five trustees of the trust fund that Wallace set up to handle financial gifts to his relatives. He is the only one of the five trustees who is not a member of the Wallace family. Besides giving Wallace the benefit of his advice on editorial policies and handling special promotion jobs, such as the successful one years ago on an article called '—And Sudden Death,' Dudley also suggests ideas for *Digest* articles and recommends editorial talent. Dudley also helps Wallace keep the *Digest* free of individuals whom Dudley regards as dangerous radicals. He is, as you can see, a valuable man, and he has considerable power around the *Digest*."

As a result of listening to all this, I miss several rounds of toasts, but there are many more, and I down one glass of unsweetened grapefruit juice after another. There are peanut-butter sandwiches for those who care for them, but no champagne and no caviar, either beluga or sevruga. Small wonder, perhaps, that when I take my leave of the land of *The Reader's Digest,* I find myself repeating that old American saying, "It's a nice place to visit, but I wouldn't want to live there."

5

ELEVEN MILLION COPIES, INCLUDING THE SCANDINAVIAN

IN THE past twenty-four years, *The Reader's Digest,* which started out as a little magazine printing second-hand literature, has become one of the biggest things in publishing. The foundation of its great strength is its wide public appeal. Since the magazine has always shown a conspicuous coyness about the true state of its circulation, the grand total of eleven million copies a month that it now acknowledges may be a quite modest understatement. The figure is, nevertheless, staggering. No other magazine anywhere in the world has ever done half so well. Approximately nine and a half million copies of the *Digest* are printed in English. Of these, seven million are sold in the United States and Canada. The production of the domestic edition, one of the larger printing jobs of our time, is divided between the Rumford Press, in

Concord, New Hampshire, and the R. R. Donnelly & Sons Company, in Chicago. The Canadian edition is printed in Montreal. A British edition, started in 1937 and printed in London, has a circulation of two hundred and twenty-five thousand, more than that of any other one-shilling magazine. During the war, the *Digest* published four special editions which followed the troops. These were printed in Egypt, Australia, India, and France for troops in the Mediterranean, Pacific, China-Burma-India, and European war theaters. Their combined circulation was over two million copies, or roughly one for every seventh American in uniform. Copies for the armed forces were supplied at half price. This bargain rate was offered to ex-service men and women for the two years following the war, in order, the magazine announced, "to make sure that *The Reader's Digest* need not be denied them during the period of their readjustment to civilian life."

Having converted a large segment of the adult citizenry, the *Digest* is now engaged in proselytizing the youth of the nation. It puts out a special version for children, called the school, or expurgated, edition. It is the same as the trade, or unexpurgated, edition, except that it does not include the articles on sex or the off-color jokes which occasionally appear in the regular edition. The school edition, which is sold for fifteen cents a copy to students in high schools, to use mostly in English classes, has a sixteen-page section containing questions and study forms intended to help the novices master the material. The circulation of the school edition is over six hundred thousand copies a month; this is more than the combined circulations of the *Atlantic Monthly,* the *New Republic, Harper's,* the *Nation,* the *American Mercury,* and *Fortune.* The *Digest,* alone among major magazines, is available not only to everyone who has eyes to see but also to those who haven't. It is the only major magazine published in Braille. Even the blind who can't read Braille are not shut off from the *Digest.* For them the *Digest* is inscribed every month on phonograph records and distributed in what is called the talking-record edition. The *Digest* can thus be absorbed by anyone in this country who has command of his sense of sight, touch, or hearing.

People in other countries are not quite so fortunate; they have to be able to read a little in order to enjoy the *Digest*. The magazine had considered entering the Latin-American market as early as 1936, but it did not begin the invasion until four years later, when it put out a Spanish-language edition, *Selecciones del Reader's Digest*. Published in Cuba and distributed in all Spanish-speaking Latin-American countries and in Spain, *Selecciones* has a circulation of eight hundred and fifty thousand a month; it is the largest-selling Spanish-language magazine in the world. A Portuguese-language edition, *Seleções do Reader's Digest*, was started in 1942. *Seleções* is now bought every month by three hundred and ten thousand customers in Brazil, Portugal, and Portuguese East and West Africa. It is the largest-selling Portuguese-language magazine in the world. In 1943, the *Digest* entered two other markets. In the spring it started a Swedish edition, *Det Bästa ur Reader's Digest*, which is published in Stockholm and has a circulation of two hundred and seventy-five thousand. *Det Bästa* is the largest-selling Swedish-language monthly magazine in the world. That summer, an Arabic-language edition, *Al Mukhtar min Reader's Digest*, made its début in Egypt. It is printed in Cairo, is bought every

month by a hundred and twenty-five thousand na-
tives in Egypt, Syria, Palestine, Lebanon, Iraq,
Transjordan, and Saudi Arabia, and is the largest-selling Finnish-language magazine in the
A Finnish edition, *Valitut Palap Reader's Digest
'Ista,* which was started in June, 1945, has a circulation of one hundred thousand and is the largest-selling Arabic-language magazine in the world.
world. The *Digest's* thirteenth special, and sixth
foreign-language, edition appeared in March,
1946, in Denmark. The Danish edition, *Det Bedste
fra Reader's Digest,* which got under way with a
printing of one hundred and sixty thousand copies, will undoubtedly become the largest-selling
Danish-language magazine in the world. All the
Digest's foreign editions consist of translations
of articles that have appeared in the domestic edition. In Carson City or Copenhagen, the *Digest* is
a standardized product, and apparently is inter-
nationally irresistible.

In its onward and upward course, *The Reader's
Digest* has been aided by the collaboration of most
of the well-known magazines. By giving Wallace
their old articles, they made it possible for the
magazine which Wallace used to call The Little

Aristocrat to exist in the first place. They have
continued their support, even though the erst-
while little aristocrat is now big enough to take
care of itself. The *Digest* is today so well off that
it can afford to help many of its less successful
old friends in a financial way by distributing a
large sum of money among them every year and
in an editorial way by giving them all the
ready-made articles they can use free of charge.
The *Digest* is prepared to work its way considerably further onto the editorial premises of other
magazines, as the editor of a periodical which will
here be called *Gray's Review* discovered during
the war. The editor of that venerable magazine
wanted to send a well-known writer across the
country to prepare a series of articles about certain aspects of wartime America, but he hesitated
because the traveling expenses involved were large
and the magazine's editorial budget was small. He
had the happy idea of asking assistance from the
Digest and wrote Wallace a letter outlining the
project. Wallace replied with a pleasant note giving his implied approval, along with a check for
several hundred dollars. That *Gray's Review* and
probably some other magazines are on chummy

terms with the *Digest* seems clear from the experience of a writer who was asked to take over the writing of one of the departments in *Gray's Review*. The writer was interviewed not by the editor of *Gray's Review*, as he had naturally expected, but by a representative of the *Digest*. When the discussion got around to money, the *Digest* man said that the job would pay seven hundred dollars a month, three hundred dollars of which would be paid by *Gray's Review* and the balance by the *Digest*. The *Digest* has consistently denied rumors that it owns stock in other magazines, and these denials are believable. It is as unnecessary for the little aristocrat to risk capital in other periodicals, so long as they continue to be so obliging, as it would be for a big aristocrat like a king to ask his subjects for a deed to his palace.

In addition to exercising a benevolent, unofficial suzerainty over magazine publishers, the *Digest* is moving toward a situation in which it may one day enjoy the same relationship with book publishers. In nearly every issue, the *Digest* prints a condensation of a book, usually a new one. Many publishers are convinced that a *Digest* condensation aids the sale of a book, and accordingly make a practice of sending the *Digest* advance proofs of books in which they think the magazine might be interested. If the book looks promising to the *Digest*, the magazine may take an option on the condensation rights; it has paid as much as three thousand dollars for this privilege. If the book is used, the *Digest* makes the publisher another substantial payment, a share of which goes to the author. The amount the *Digest* pays for book-condensation rights varies, but it probably seldom falls below five thousand dollars, and may be considerably more. It is at least enough to excite the interest of many publishers to the point of doing business with the *Digest* and to make closer ties between the *Digest* and book publishers highly probable. As one eminent publisher has baldly observed, "They pay so much money, you can't resist."

Although many magazine editors and publishers have become privately critical of the *Digest*, nearly all are publicly neutral toward it and professionally in favor of it. This is curious, for it would seem to mean that the majority of magazine people are in favor of assisting a magazine which is their competitor. As the *Digest* now goes into the open market to commission writers to do a large number of its articles, it must necessarily compete with other magazines in buying editorial material. This fact of publishing life, still apparently not known to some magazine editors, was brought home bluntly not long ago to the editors of *Life*. Before Eric Johnston, then president of the United States Chamber of Commerce, made his widely advertised trip to the Soviet Union in the spring of 1944, *Life* arranged to buy an article which he planned to write about his Russian experiences. The morning after Johnston's return to this country, two editors of *Life* visited him in his suite at the Waldorf. "My, this has been a busy morning," Johnston said as he greeted them. "Mr. Wallace of the *Digest* just this minute left." Mr. Wallace, Johnston went on, had offered him twenty-five thousand dollars for an article about his interview with Stalin. "I told Mr. Wallace it wasn't worth that much," Johnston modestly added, "but he said, 'It's worth that much to us.'" *Life* evidently hadn't figured on the possibility of Johnston's writing two Russian articles. Having lost the very desirable Stalin piece to their competitors, the *Life* editors had to be satisfied with taking another article by Johnston about Russia; this turned out to be good Johnston but hardly twenty-five-grand Johnston. Wallace later confirmed his high opinion of Johnston the journalist by giving him a bonus of fifteen thousand dollars for Christmas. When it was announced, some time after the Johnston episode, that Heinrich Himmler had conferred with Count Folke Bernadotte about a possible surrender, an enterprising editor of *Life* quickly cabled one of the magazine's European representatives to get in touch with the Count and offer him a large sum for a story about the Himmler conferences. The Count cabled his answer to *Life's* New York office. He said he would like to write the piece for *Life,* but unfortunately he had already been signed up to do it for *The Reader's Digest.*

An additional indication of the *Digest's* position as a competitor is contained in the following excerpt from a letter written by one of the *Digest's* Senior Editors to the editor of a popular magazine who had asked why the *Digest* was currently reprinting only a niggardly number of articles from his magazine:

Each month we send a questionnaire to 4,000 subscribers, seeking to learn what they like and don't like in the current issue. The final report for July, before me as I write, shows that the first fifteen articles in point of popularity were all originated in this office. The reader, of course, doesn't know what we place and what we find.

I hope you won't think us conceited. . . . Believe me when I say that our people would much rather find articles than create them. But they do have their likes and dislikes. . . .

Since, as the letter points out, *Digest* editors can no longer find in other magazines articles which they believe will be popular with their readers, the *Digest* has had to go into the business of manufacturing its own brand of articles. These are unique. *Digest* articles are as peculiar to the *Digest* as *Saturday Evening Post* articles are to the *Post* or *Life* articles to *Life*. This peculiarity, this uniqueness, is what *Digest* readers like. *Digest* articles are so clearly different from articles found in other magazines that *Digest* fans, as the Senior Editor remarks, can somehow sense them, even when they have been planted in some other periodical and later appear in the *Digest* blandly disguised as reprints. The millions do not buy the *Digest* to read an occasional article created, say, by the *Saturday Evening Post* and reprinted by the *Digest*. If they liked *Post* articles best, they would buy the *Post*. Whether they know it or not, the millions buy the *Digest* because they prefer articles created by the *Digest*. It may well be that *The Reader's Digest* today is just another magazine in the market place, in competition with other magazines which have so solicitously fostered its growth.

During the war, most of the *Digest's* competitors had to limit their circulation because of the world paper shortage. The *Digest* kept right on growing. Toward the end of 1943, when the paper problem had already become so acute that getting on the subscription rolls of almost any important magazine had become something like getting tapped for Skull and Bones, the *Digest* put on a big subscription drive. Evidently having all kinds of paper to spare, the *Digest* pursued its prospects unrelentingly with brochures sent first-class mail and sometimes even by air mail and special delivery. A poor relation asking for money could scarcely have been more persistent. The government authorities apparently were not altogether heedless of the *Digest's* requests for extra allotments of paper. They were also quite decent about assisting the *Digest's* wartime expansion abroad. For example, to facilitate the establishment of *Al Mukhtar min Reader's Digest,* the Arabic edition, the Office of War Information in 1943 arranged for the *Digest's* general manager, A. L. Cole, and its assistant general manager, Fred D. Thompson, Jr., to become O.W.I. employees. The Messrs. Cole and Thompson, enjoying a technical status as publishing consultants to the O.W.I., without pay, were provided with priorities, while the war was still in progress, to travel to Egypt and transact their business in connection with *Al Mukhtar.* The State Department has also been helpful. As Mr. Cole once explained to a government official, "The State Department transmits through diplomatic pouch each month by air to Cairo the necessary material for the reproduction of this magazine [*Al Mukhtar*] and has every month since it was started."

In addition to expanding its foreign and domestic editions during the war, the *Digest* also enlarged its extra-curricular activities, including its Reprint Department, which distributes, at a cost of a couple of cents each in lots of a hundred or more, reprints of some of the more memorable *Digest* articles. In its earlier days, the Reprint Department offered such varied titles as "The Menace of Huey Long" and "Breast Feeding for Babies." In recent times, however, it has concentrated on political pieces of a militantly conservative nature, such as "Boondoggling on a Global Basis," by Henry J. Taylor; "Don't Blame the Bureaucrat!," by Representative Hatton W. Sumners; and "Road to Serfdom," by Friedrich Hayek. Reprints of Hayek's work, which has been called the reactionaries' Manifesto, were made available, as the *Digest* phrased it, "through the courtesy of the Book-of-the-Month Club."

To spread the *Digest* message to two other less literate but enormous audiences, Wallace, in 1944, turned to the movies and to the radio. In the fall of that year, *Variety* reported that Wallace, who had previously considered and discarded several projected plans for adapting *Digest* material to the films, had finally closed a deal with Metro-

Goldwyn-Mayer to produce a series of eight short features based on original *Digest* articles. At about the same time, Wallace also got the *Digest* involved in two radio programs. One, an item called *"The Reader's Digest*—Radio Edition," and sponsored by Hall Brothers, Inc., greeting-card manufacturers, is a half-hour show featuring dramatizations, the announcer says, "of the fascinating material found in *The Reader's Digest.*" This is broadcast weekly over a hundred and forty-seven stations of the Columbia Broadcasting System. Wallace's other excursion into radio was somewhat more ambitious. In 1944, he signed a one-year contract to sponsor an hour-long show called "Town Meeting of the Air," which had been a popular sustaining program since 1935. This program, on which eminent citizens debate popular issues and submit to questioning and heckling by members of the audience, is intended to give an airing to both sides of controversial questions. That the Town Meeting program could be bought by any commercial sponsor caused some surprise in radio circles. During the previous nine years of its existence, it had adamantly turned down all offers of commercial sponsorship in order, as a *Digest* article about the show once explained, "to keep the program on an unbiased basis." This piece, one of a brace of adulatory articles the *Digest* did about the show, added that officials of the program had the "feeling that the hour would defeat its purpose if it had anything to sell but truth" and went on to quote a Texas farmer who regularly listened to the show and who said, "I hope to God it don't end up in some kind of propaganda." Some of the *Digest's* severer critics came to the hasty conclusion that the farmer's fears began to be realized after the *Digest* took over the program. They felt that the show was subtly arranged, through the selection of speakers and a practice of planting questions in the audience, so that the *Digest's* extremely conservative point of view was made to predominate. The Town Meeting management denied these charges, explaining that the program was not rigged and that it was as free from outside influence as it had been before the *Digest* took over as its sponsor. Wallace withdrew the *Digest's* sponsorship of the program in the fall of 1945.

Even if the producers of the Town Meeting program had planted questions in the audience, they would simply have been using a system the *Digest* recommends to some fifteen thousand other discussion groups which subscribe to the *Digest's* Program Service, another of the magazine's manifold extra-curricular projects. The Program Service is a package deal by which the *Digest*, for the sum of a dollar a year, supplies luncheon and ladies' clubs, Kiwanians and Rotarians, and other groups with material for holding meetings to discuss topical issues. The program material, sent to subscribers every month except during the summer, is based mainly on *Digest* articles, and is a slick and standardized product. A typical outline for a *Digest*-planned meeting includes a ready-made speech which the chairman can use to open the meeting, prepared remarks to be delivered by parties identified as first, second, third, and fourth speakers, and a chairman's hand-me-down summary. The material also includes "Suggested Questions" to be asked from the floor; these are printed on a perforated sheet of paper so that they can be torn off and distributed among members of the group who are unable to think up questions of their own but want to get into the act. A recent outline distributed by the

Program Service was devoted to a discussion of China. To prepare for this meeting, the chairman was briefed as follows:

> Invite several members of a Chinese family in your own community to come to the meeting. . . . Ask them to wear native dress, to bring their writing materials, their chopsticks, and the bowls from which they eat, their cooking utensils, or anything else which will illustrate the simple details of Chinese daily life.

The instructions, acknowledging by indirection that it may not be easy to find a Chinese sufficiently exhibitionistic to participate in the program, tell the chairman not to get downcast. "Do not overlook the possibilities in your neighborhood Chinese," the booklet says. "He may be a humble man—a gardener, a laundryman, or a small businessman." Assuming that the chairman has been successful in bagging a local laundryman and he has shown up with a suitable collection of pots, pans, and chopsticks, the leader can then look under "Procedure of the Meeting" to find out what to do next:

Open with an informal period of perhaps thirty minutes during which you, as host, introduce your Chinese guests, give everyone a chance to become better acquainted with them, and provide opportunity for them to demonstrate native Chinese customs—way of writing, use of chopsticks, etc.—and to explain the exhibits to your members.

After the laundryman has finished his act, everything else goes like clockwork. "Limit each speaker to ten minutes," the chairman is advised, and then is told to warn the speakers not to start talking any deep stuff—"to stick closely to the homely facts of life, resisting with discrimination and self-control the tempting labyrinths of Chinese history and politics." When the first, second, and other speakers have run through their routines, the time comes for questions from the floor. A member of the audience, who has been supplied with a "suggested question" to be addressed to the first speaker, gets up and says, "Do Chinese men to-day still wear the traditional Chinese gown? How about women?" After this is answered, a party with a question for the second speaker rises to ask,

"What familiar table delicacies have we inherited from the Chinese?" Difficult though these questions may seem, the first and second speakers will not be stumped, inasmuch as they have had an opportunity to see the questions in advance and to look up the answers in the recommended reading. If the meeting is handled according to directions on the Program Service booklet, it can be run off in one hour flat.

Since *The Reader's Digest* has now become a way of life, it may be instructive to visualize an American home which makes use of all the facilities the *Digest* provides. Father is reading the current edition of the *Digest* while Mother is tuned in to the *Digest* radio program. Brother, just home from the Army, is finishing his overseas edition. Sister is upstairs in her room studying her school edition. (She will sneak Father's unexpurgated edition up to her room when she gets a chance.) Uncle is at the movies watching a *Digest* feature. Aunt, who has found a few reprints of "The Menace of Huey Long" lying around the house, is busy mailing them out to friends. Grandfather, who has lost his sight, is enjoying the Braille edition, while Grandmother, also blind but unable to read Braille, is sitting in her room taking in the Talking-Book edition by ear. In the kitchen, Cook is poring over *Det Bästa*. In the evening, the family will gather in the living room to welcome some neighbors, who will be coming over to take part in a meeting based on the Program Service material. After the laundryman, carrying his chopsticks and other props, pads in, the meeting will get under way. By exercising discrimination and self-control, the participants may be able to avoid the tempting labyrinths of a thoughtful discussion.

6

DR. WALLACE'S MAGIC FORMULA

DeWITT WALLACE is regarded by many of his colleagues in the magazine business with the awesome respect that members of the American Chemical Society might accord a precocious youth who had discovered the formula for transmuting base metal into gold. Though he had no newspaper or magazine experience, Wallace twenty-four years ago discovered the journalistic philosopher's stone, the formula that has made *The Reader's Digest* the most successful magazine in history. Naturally, he has been reluctant to reveal his magic formula. When asked about it, he usually replies, as he did a while ago to Kenneth Stewart, a writer for *PM*, in misty generalities: "Primarily, we are looking for articles of lasting interest which will appeal to a large audience, articles that come within the range of interests, experience, and conversation of the average person. The over-all emphasis ... has been a more or less conscious effort to promote a Better America, with capital letters, with a fuller life for all, and with a place for the United States of increasing influence and respect in world affairs.'' These remarks, which sound more like a political-campaign speech than a sober, scientific statement, give Wallace's colleagues few clues, for all they reveal is that his magazine's success is a result of its practice of printing articles of lasting interest. They do not answer the basic question: What is an article of lasting interest? Perhaps neither Wallace nor anyone else can answer that question definitely, because whether an article is of lasting or only passing interest depends, of course, on the person who reads it. People who were impressed by such *Digest* articles as ''Does Being an Old Maid Hurt?,'' ''Higher Education of the Silkworm,'' ''Has the Ku Klux Klan the Right to Celebrate Christmas?,'' and ''$40,000 for a Hog—How Much for Your Child?'' would probably find them of as much interest today as they did when they appeared twenty years ago. The article called ''God Is *Still* Undiscovered'' surely has as much appeal today as it had when it

was printed in 1923. Yet the passage of time is
bound to affect certain articles. Readers who several years ago enjoyed pieces like "President Cool-
idge's Efficiency," "The Hair-Net Industry of
North China," and "I Could Make This Country
Bone-Dry" (by Pussyfoot Johnson) might now
find them, to use the variant of the *Digest* slogan
devised by the editors of the *Yale Record*, "articles lacking interest."

Although Wallace does not talk about the *Digest*
formula, its primary ingredients can be identified
by analysis. This is not an arduous process. One
important ingredient, for example, was discovered
by a magazine editor in reading a single issue of
the *Digest*. Having been invited to meet Wallace
at lunch, the editor felt obligated to become acquainted with his host's magazine. He bought a
copy, read it through, and then said, "Sounds like
some goddam preacher wrote it." This offhand
summary is not far from the truth: Wallace, whose
family and editorial staff are sprinkled with
preachers, has an evangelical streak visible at a
hundred yards. The ingredient in the *Digest* formula isolated by this analysis is Optimism, with,
as Wallace might say, a capital letter. The quality

of optimism in *The Reader's Digest* is not strained. It drips from every issue as sweetly as syrup from a maple tree. It is a brave and tender philosophy that has been well stated in "The Optimist's Creed," displayed in the Mayflower Doughnut Shops, which adjures all wayfarers through life, whatever may be their goal, to keep their eye upon the doughnut and not upon the hole. Because of the *Digest's* rampant optimism, which recognizes evil and misfortune only as manifestations of the Almighty's wisdom, or as blessings in disguise, it has always been warmly acclaimed by large sections of the clergy. Dr. Douglas Buchanan, D.D., of the First Presbyterian Church in Kansas City, some years ago put the clergy's collective thought succinctly into words when he wrote the publication that it is "a gold mine of sermonic material for the up-to-date minister."

A minister, or any other prospector, who digs into the *Digest* will be almost certain to discover more nuggets of optimism than he can bear. The *Digest* is able to find something good to say about nearly every aspect of life, from birth to death, inclusive. For example, the *Digest* on childbirth:

I regard my initial experience in maternity as the intoxicating experience of my life, of an act in the drama more soul-satisfying than any other. And presumably I am a normal woman.

On the human race:

Yet a healthy perspective on history gives convincing testimony that human nature has changed, and is changing, for the better. . . . Sometimes we are conscious only of dissonant jealousies, greeds, and hatred. But after a survey of the good old days, even the cynical observer admits that the leopard's spots *have* changed, and that human beings are not the ornery, cross-grained, calloused creatures they used to be.

This was written in 1941, some time before the discovery of Buchenwald and Belsen, but even the atrocities committed in those two concentration camps are not necessarily a cause for pessimism. What you think of people, the *Digest* has explained, depends on how you look at them. Thus:

People may seem to be perfectly impossible. They may seem mean and small and sly. But if you will take ten paces to the left and look again with the light falling at a different angle, very likely you will see that they are generous and warm and kind.

On racial problems:

As a Negro, I am vastly encouraged by the changes in the South during the past two decades in race relations, education, health, and business—all indications of a new day breaking for my people in Dixie.

On the future of mankind:

However, geneticists, on the basis of solid science, hold forth a glorious picture for the future. They tell us that, by improving our environment and our heredity simultaneously, we could in a few generations abolish nearly all human afflictions.

On old age:

Life now is not so rapturous, but it is vastly more interesting.

On sickness:

> If you have never been sick, never lost so
> much as a day in bed—then you have missed
> something! When your turn comes, don't be
> dismayed. Remind yourself that pain and suf-
> fering may teach you something valuable. . . .
> Possibly it may change for the better the
> entire course of your life.

On death:

> Someday you are going to die and, if you're
> like most of us, you are probably afraid to
> die; you believe that death will be unpleasant.
> In that you are wrong. It is not unpleasant to
> die.

The *Digest,* looking at everything from the cra-
dle to the grave through rose-colored spectacles
rosier than any heretofore known to optical science, has probably never been more shrilly optimistic than in an article about a couple whose
second child turned out to be a Mongolian idiot.
The mother, keeping her eye firmly on the silver
lining, wrote an article for the *Digest* about this

tragedy. "After all," she said in the course of it, "agony can be made to count for something."

No matter how complicated the issue discussed in a *Digest* article may be, the article contains nothing that cannot be grasped readily by a high-school student of average ability. There are no hard words. There are no difficult ideas. The articles read like stories in a primer. This quality results from the second ingredient in the *Digest* formula, an ingredient that may handily be called Simplism. This is the element that gives all *Digest* articles the appearance, if not the actual quality, of simplicity. The difference between simplicity and simplism is something like the difference between sterling and plated silver. The presence of simplism can be readily detected in the finished product. Take a *Digest* article on taxes which says, "To dodge complications which might easily drive you crazy, think simply of all taxes as falling into two classes." Dodging complications is a form of simplism. Sometimes the *Digest* uses another form of simplism. This consists merely of saying that something is "simple," and is based on the theory that saying a thing is simple makes it so. For example, in a piece on the renegotiation of war contracts, the *Digest* remarked, "The way to handle this problem is simple." Neither of these methods will take care of all problems, of course, but by using some version or other of the simplistic method, the *Digest* can turn out an article on a difficult scientific or economic topic so that it appears to be as simple as the hair-net industry of North China. Dodging a few complications, the *Digest* once explained the profit system in a three-page article written in the form of a letter from a presumably sage old man to his adolescent grandson, who had become "disturbed by the current fashion of speaking disparagingly of the profit system" and had asked his grandfather to relieve his mind. "My dear Grandson," the grandfather began, "I will answer your question as simply as I can." He did.

Another easily identifiable element in the *Digest* formula is Dogmatism. The proportion of this ingredient in the formula has increased in recent years. When the *Digest* was younger, divergent opinions circulated quite freely through its pages. As the magazine has aged, it has become afflicted with what one observer has diagnosed as hardening of the articles. The publication shows marked symptoms of bias on many subjects, most noticeably government and labor. The dogmatism in the *Digest* results from three editorial practices. First, though it still purports to be a balanced synthesis of the published word, it prints more unfavorable than favorable articles about certain subjects; its articles on the domestic policies of the Roosevelt Administration are an example. Second, by never printing a correction, the *Digest* surrounds itself with an aura of infallibility. In the February, 1944, issue the *Digest* ran a testy article called " 'You Can't Pay Workers That Much,' " which, in the opinion of Secretary of the Treasury Morgenthau, contained such a startling number of errors that he felt it necessary to point them out in a five-page letter. "I am sure you will agree with me," the Secretary said, "that your readers deserve to know the facts." Evidently the *Digest* did not agree, for it printed nothing more on the topic. The third *Digest* practice that leads to dogmatism is a frequently employed one known as the hard-working-author technique. It results in the frequent appearance in *Digest* articles of such passages as "From 553 single-spaced pages, I cite the following typical incidents," "This article is based in part on a six-years' research," and "I asked two hundred people what they did to cure a cold." All these touches are intended to convince the reader that the author has labored so mightily that his findings can be accepted as The Word.

The most important ingredient in the *Digest* formula is, of course, Wallace himself. His talent is the catalyst that causes the elements of optimism, simplism, and dogmatism to combine in such a way that they produce articles of lasting interest. During the past twenty-four years, Wallace's magic formula has been applied to more than nine thousand articles. He apparently considers some of these perfect examples of the article of lasting interest. These are the repeaters—the articles which the *Digest* has printed twice. In the June, 1944, issue of the *Digest,* there appeared such a repeater, an article, written by Hanson Baldwin, called " 'The Titanic Is Unsinkable.' " Precisely the same article, except for three fewer commas and one different word, had been printed in the *Digest* before, as the lead story in the issue of March, 1934. Contrary to what some innocent *Digest* readers might suspect, Baldwin did not submit and sell the article to the *Digest* twice. Nor was the repetition, which would be considered almost as gauche as knowing plagiarism by most magazines, the result of editorial negligence. It was deliberate.

From time to time, when Wallace recalls an old *Digest* story that especially pleased him, he orders it dug up and printed again. Not all *Digest* articles can be successfully exhumed. Wallace has published scores of articles on science, but so far he has not deemed a single one in this category deserving of a repeat performance. He has also vetoed all of the hundreds of *Digest* articles on international affairs, education, agriculture, sports, war, birth control, juvenile delinquency, civics, the movies, and religion. Many of them, written by such notable persons as the late Wendell Willkie, Sumner Welles, Senator Vandenberg, Eleanor Roosevelt, Edward Stettinius, Eric Johnston, and Henry Wallace, are widely regarded as useful, balanced, and in some instances admirable. But Wallace evidently considers articles in all these groups as imperfect examples of articles of lasting interest. To judge by the repeaters, there are six categories of articles which, in Wallace's expert opinion, rank highest in the quality of endurance. First are those which come under the broad heading of "Book of Knowledge" articles, such as the piece about the Titanic.[1] Second are crusading articles.[2] Wallace also includes articles on potentially controversial topics,[3] articles on animals,[4] articles on health and medicine,[5] and articles on the art of living.[6] To view a cross-section of the *Digest,* one can perhaps do nothing

[1] Other examples: "Where Do We Get Our Prejudices?," October, 1926, and March, 1937; "What Makes People Laugh?," March, 1922, and April, 1927.

[2] Example: "Don't Growl—Kick!," which admonished *Digest* readers to rise and take action against injustices like tipping and unpleasant salesclerks, published originally in February, 1922, and repeated in April, 1927. An article with the same title, treating the same theme, but written by another author, turned up in the December, 1934, *Digest.*

[3] Example: "Can We Have a Beautiful Race?," published in February, 1922, and revived in September, 1926. The article, which was concerned with the touchy topic of immigration, said that we can develop a beautiful race of human beings in this country if we stop letting into the country immigrant women who are "flat-chested with necks like a prize fighter and with faces as expressionless and devoid of beauty as a pumpkin."

[4] Examples: "The Firefly's Light," February, 1922, and October, 1926; "When Spiders Fly," March, 1922, and February, 1928.

[5] Examples: "That Tired Feeling," September, 1922, and October, 1924; "Confessions of a Sun Worshipper," August, 1929, and September, 1938; "The Sanity of Insanity," June, 1935, and August, 1943.

[6] Such as: "Footnotes to a Happy Marriage," published originally in August, 1932, and repeated in September, 1939; "To Bore or Not to Bore," February, 1922, and March, 1927; "A Sabbatical Year for Marriage," January, 1928, and November, 1941.

better than examine these six important categories.

The "Book of Knowledge" category of articles contains a large assortment of miscellaneous facts. For example, the number of hairs on the human head varies from 88,000 for redheads to 102,000 for brunettes and 104,000 for blondes. The article doesn't say why. Since the Age of Steam (circa 1750), the population of the earth has more than tripled: from 660,000,000 to over 2,100,000,000. Dehydrated soups were used in the Boer War. About 6,000 stars are visible to the unaided eye, though no more than half at any given time. In China, there is only one college student for every 10,000 citizens, while in the District of Columbia, dairy farmers are given demerits if they do not wipe each cow's udders with a separate towel. The self-propelling torpedo was invented in 1864. Seventy-five years later, there were 13,000,000 known drug addicts in the four northeastern provinces of China. The average Jap lives to the age of forty-eight. Americans hang on to about sixty-four, despite the fact that ninety-seven per cent of the bread they eat is white.

Although all this information gives the *Digest's*

readers something to think about, the material involved just doesn't permit the articles to become
as red-hot as those in the crusading category.
"We pride ourselves," DeWitt Wallace once declared, "on being a little more fearless than any
other magazine published." The *Digest* has
printed many fearless articles in support of the
campaign to stamp out syphilis, in favor of safe
driving, sponsoring the Sister Kenny method of
treating infantile paralysis, and advancing such
causes as cheaper milk and the suppression of
filthy magazines. In years past, the *Digest* has
also printed numerous articles that disapproved
of advertising, but the magazine's attitude toward
the profession has in recent times become noticeably more mellow. In advertising circles it is regarded as not altogether coincidental that the
change occurred at about the time the *Digest*
began putting out its foreign editions, most of
which carry forty-four pages of advertisements,
providing the company with an annual revenue of
approximately a million and a half dollars. However, the *Digest* still does not accept cigarette
advertising, or any other kind, in its domestic
edition. Starting with his first issue, which con-

tained a warning that "one cigarette will kill a cat," Wallace, who smokes around two packs of cigarettes a day, has conducted an unrelenting anti-cigarette crusade. One memorable article in this series was written by a man who told how much better he felt after giving up the cigarette habit. Four months later he killed himself. The *Digest* nevertheless continued to condemn cigarettes. Its July, 1942, issue carried an article called "Cigarette Ad Fact and Fiction," which denounced cigarette advertising as silly and misleading. It told of tests sponsored by the *Digest* which showed that all the leading brands of cigarettes contained such harmful ingredients as nicotine and tars in about equal amounts. Old Golds, however, contained a tiny bit less than any of the others, the story said. Although its margin of superiority was spectacularly infinitesimal, Old Gold republished the findings in full-page newspaper ads, which announced, "READER'S DIGEST EXPOSES CIGARETTE CLAIMS! . . . Impartial Tests Find Old Gold *Lowest* in *Nicotine* and *Throat-Irritating* Tars and Resins. . . . Get July Reader's Digest. Turn to page 5. See what this highly respected magazine reports." The sale of Old Golds improved handsomely.

The *Digest* put on one of its most ambitious crusades in 1941. This one was against untrustworthy automobile, radio, and watch repairmen. The magazine sent two investigators, a writer named John Patric and his secretary, Miss Lioy May, across the country in a second-hand twelve-cylinder Lincoln Zephyr which had been overhauled and put in excellent condition beforehand. Their method of operation was this: Upon entering a town, Mr. Patric would disconnect an ignition wire, so that the engine would operate on only six cylinders instead of twelve. Then, while he waited around a corner, Miss May would drive into a garage, pretending she didn't know what was wrong with the car, and ask to have it repaired. Then, taking a radio in which a tube had been deliberately loosened and a watch whose crown wheel had been slightly tinkered with, Miss May would play the same game with a local radio man and watch repairman. The two *Digest* operatives spent three months and drove 14,516 miles in making their investigation, the results of which were revealed in a series of three articles. What they found out was that the repairmen, more often than not, knavishly overcharged Miss May. This disclosure, while interesting, was not altogether surprising. Some readers reacted to the *Digest's* exposé as calmly as George Bernard Shaw did when told of Pavlov's laborious discovery that a dog's mouth waters when he hears the dinner bell. "If the fellow had come to me," Shaw said, "I could have given him that information in less than twenty-five seconds without tormenting a single dog."

However peculiar some *Digest* crusades may seem, they are motivated by the best intentions. The magazine is interested in good works. It even suffers at times from a malady which could be called—to quote a phrase Bruce Barton used in a *Digest* article about President Roosevelt—"the intolerance of the well-doer." "Nobody can be quite so intolerant," Barton said, "no one can so cheerfully sow such seeds of violent hate as he who is completely convinced of his own self-righteousness." What Barton said is applicable to the *Digest*, too. The *Digest* is so eager to do the right thing that it sometimes seems to deviate

from the golden mean of impartiality in handling
certain topics in the potentially-controversial category. That the *Digest,* like any other publication,
has a right to exploit a partisan point of view on
any subject has never been questioned, but there
appears to be some doubt whether it is altogether
sporting of a magazine to grind an editorial axe
while pretending to be a literary cross-section.

The *Digest* is often accused of being anti-labor.
It has often claimed that it isn't. "None of our
articles has been anti-labor," a *Digest* spokesman
said publicly not long ago. During the seven years
from 1939 through 1945, the *Digest* printed seven-
ty-six articles on labor. The great majority of
these do not prove anything, one way or the other,
about the *Digest's* attitude toward labor. By and
large, they discuss aspects of the labor question
that are outside the controversial area. For example, there have been many punchy little essays
which show conclusively that if labor and management would stop knocking each other, shake hands,
and begin playing four-square, this would be a
happier world by a darned sight. Other *Digest*
articles have arrived at the profound conclusion
that workers like to be treated like human beings.

Another has imparted the news that labor and management get along pretty well together in Sweden. Another has come out strongly in favor of building churches near factories as a convenience for the workingman. The *Digest* has also published several biographical sketches of successful labor leaders. These are collectively as noncommittal as *Who's Who,* with the exception of one piece about Andrew Furuseth, the noted head of the International Seamen's Union. The *Digest* went overboard for Furuseth. It called the piece about him "Saint Andrew the Sailor." This was not as deliriously pro-labor as it might seem, as Furuseth had died a year before the piece was printed and had in fact been almost universally regarded as a saintly man. Altogether, from 1939 through 1945, the *Digest* printed sixty labor articles that successfully skirt that area of the labor question which is still controversial.

In the same period, the *Digest* printed sixteen articles about unions. If, as many people believe, an attitude toward unions is a fair index of an attitude toward labor, then the *Digest's* views on labor become quite clear from what it has printed. One of the articles on unions is about a plant in which eighteen unions work together in harmony; another is about a school run by the National Maritime Union to train its members for leadership. A third is a complimentary article about the Typographical Union, described by the *Digest* as a model for all labor organizations—a reasonable choice, since the Typographical Union, being the oldest union in America, has passed through its rough-and-tumble days and settled down into sedate respectability. With these three exceptions, the sixteen *Digest* articles concerned directly with unions were plainly and extensively unfavorable. With notable consistency, writers of such *Digest* articles take the not entirely disarming stand that they are so eager to help that it hurts them more than it does the unions to administer such a thrashing.

"It is not because I want to weaken them," William Hard, a reformed *New Republic* writer who has become a *Digest* editor and has written many of the magazine's articles on labor, has said, "that I explore the path toward union regulation. It is because I want to see the worst union local in America become as good as the best." Toward this end, Hard has felt called upon to give the worst

unions a lot of his attention. In beginning the
story of one very unseemly hodcarriers' local, the
Digest's labor expert thoughtfully pointed out
that the skulduggery about to be revealed "is a
story of a kind that has happened in local unions
in many parts of the country." Time and again he
has pointed out that "we must with equal patience
strive to purify our worst unions and to raise them
to the high moral level of our best." Hard is easily
as anxious to purify the worst unions as West-
brook Pegler is. Each, unfortunately, is so consistently preoccupied with his specialty that his
written works give the impression that all labor
leaders are racketeers and all unions are villain-
ous. The *Digest* has further covered the labor
movement by printing union articles bearing such
suggestive titles as "Must Union Members Give
Up Their American Rights?," "Remove Union
Restrictions and Increase Shipyard Production
One-Third!," and "Rehearsal for Revolution."
Other pieces have advocated state legislation
against picketing and explained the laws enacted
in Oregon to curb unions. "Our labor movement
today is in a perilous position," Hard reported in
January, 1943. "It seems to be riding high, but the

ground under it is shaking. Its friends in Congress
are diminishing and its enemies are increasing.''
It is no wonder that *Digest* readers sometimes feel
that they ought to snap out of their lethargy and
do something drastic about unions. It would seem
that the magazine does not have a prejudice
against labor but just has a prejudice against or-
ganized labor. Its position can be compared with
that of a statesman who favors freedom of the
press but opposes the use of movable type.

A while back, at a convention of the National
Council of Teachers of English, the *Digest* went
to the trouble not only of explaining its attitude
toward labor but of answering the charge that
it had also shown a distinct bias against the
Roosevelt Administration. The *Digest* spokesmen
declared that of thirty-one articles on the Administration it had printed during a particular eight-
een-month period, ''eighteen may be considered
critical of present government policies, eight
may be considered favorable to the Administration, and five may be considered neither critical
nor favorable.'' In other words, for every article
favorable to the Administration, the magazine had
printed more than two that were unfavorable. If

the analysis had been extended to include all the articles the *Digest* published on Roosevelt Administration policies from 1939 until the end of the Roosevelt era, the score would have had to be altered to three unfavorable articles for each favorable one. Neither set of figures clinches the case for the *Digest's* professed policy of impartiality.

There have also been complaints that the *Digest* is anti-Semitic and anti-Negro. In replying to the charge of anti-Semitism, the *Digest* has pointed out that some of its best articles have been written by Jews. The magazine has also pointed out that it has printed more favorable than unfavorable articles about both Jews and Negroes. These statements are quite true, but this line of reasoning has struck some observers as ingenuous, since it creates the impression that the *Digest* approaches these topics as though they were questions with two sides.

The *Digest's* policy on sex might be described as level-headed. It has, in an article by Margaret Culkin Banning, come out strongly in favor of chastity before marriage, and Gene Tunney has urged young men to practice continence. For married grownups, however, the *Digest* has presented sex information and instruction with a helpful frankness seldom seen in a family magazine. Sex is one of the features of the *Digest* articles that fall into the animal category. The *Digest* has informed its readers about the reproductive process in such animals as bears, lions, porcupines, deer, whales, echidna, and kangaroos. This is in keeping with the *Digest's* unique approach to the animal kingdom. While not yet completely convinced that the beasts in the jungle are as smart as the man in the street, the *Digest* seems to feel that the proposition has great merit. The *Digest* is perhaps the only serious magazine that has always treated talking dogs and thinking horses with respect. It has given careful consideration to a Skye terrier "able to say and understand a few words," to a Shetland pony named Black Bear that could add, subtract, do cube and square roots, and give King Solomon's dates, and to a cat named Willy who knows when it's Monday because that's the night he goes to a bingo game. That the *Digest's* anthropomorphic treatment of animals is not accidental was discovered by a naturalist who submitted a fairly dispassionate article on bears. The piece was rejected. A subordinate *Digest* editor explained to the author that Wallace had found the piece disappointing. "What Wally wants," he added, "is a story about a bear that does like that other bear we wrote about."

In an effort to induce people to send in stories about bears and other beasts that act the way Wallace wants them to, the *Digest* printed a piece in September, 1943, entitled "What Is This Wisdom of the Wild?," in which the author said, "Laboratory experimenters who subject animals to the problems of mazes and puzzles usually conclude that animals do not think. But is their conclusion correct? Isn't there, at least, an older kind of intelligence than intellect—intuition, subconscious insight, what the Indians called 'deep knowing'?" The *Digest* ended up by offering a hundred dollars to anyone who sent in an acceptable story about an "unusual example of a wild creature's 'thinking.'" Since then it has published an impressive number of pieces about wasps, woodcocks, foxes, coons, squirrels, rabbits, skunks, and other animals that act as if they possessed enough deep knowing to serve in Congress. Birds and beasts, as these

Digest contributors see them, not only think like humans, they also look and act like them. A sea otter was once described as a party "with sprucely groomed whiskers and a curiously human face which wears an expression of pleased affability. . . . He likes to float on his back. With hands crossed placidly on his breast, he bobs gently on the waves. . . . Toward his single mate he is tender and passionate . . . he caresses her with eager devotion. He lays his cheeks against hers and embraces her sleek body in his arms." As the piece goes on, the otters begin to sound suspiciously like characters in a French novel.

Wallace's views on animals are no more unusual than his views on medicine. His inclination to consider animals as bright as editors is matched by his belief that there is or soon will be a cure for all human ailments. His optimism has been reflected in *Digest* articles describing treatments or medicines that promised to improve or cure poison ivy, pneumonia, meningitis, the common cold, peritonitis, childbed fever, osteomyelitis, pellagra, cross eyes, smallpox, dementia praecox, spastic paralysis, arthritis, whooping cough, toothache, rickets, acne, cancer, leprosy, tuberculosis, heart trouble, prostate trouble, high blood pressure, dandruff, and baldness, to mention a few. Because of his admirable impatience to help mankind, Wallace tries to be the first to publish accounts of medical discoveries. Any conversations he gets into with medical men are a series of persistent questions about new treatments, experiments, and research, and he has even asked members of medical associations to give any news of such matters to the *Digest* before it is published in medical journals. He has not been successful in these efforts, and for the most part has had to content himself with publishing articles based on material that has already appeared in professional publications. This has its drawbacks, for although contributors to medical journals are notoriously conservative in the claims they make for new techniques, their initial reports are nevertheless apt to be misleading. These reports are intended primarily as a stimulus to further research rather than as definitive, final statements; frequently it is years before a new cure reaches its actual level of usefulness, and that, naturally, is often below the original expectations.

The *Digest's* interest in being first with the medical news has led to its printing such highly optimistic articles as "Hope for the Victims of Arthritis." This article, written by Paul de Kruif, who is one of the *Digest's* Roving Editors and an optimist in his own right, told of apparently impressive results obtained by treating arthritis with massive doses of Vitamin D, and particularly with a Vitamin D product called Ertron. Before winding up with the statement that "the figures bring the vision of an end to this most devastatingly crippling of all human afflictions," the author said that three doctors—Paul Magnuson, R. H. Freyberg, and Ralph Boots—were testing the treatment. After the article appeared, Dr. Boots wrote a letter to the American Medical Association *Journal,* which began:

> Paul de Kruif's enthusiastic article in this month's *Reader's Digest* entitled "Hope for the Victims of Arthritis" might better have been called "False Hope for the Victims of Arthritis."
>
> The objection which I have to the article . . . is that it stimulates great hopes in the

minds of patients with arthritis for a therapeutic agent of uncertain, if of any, permanent value, which is quite expensive, and the manufacturers of which have carried on a most intensive advertising campaign while the preparation is still on trial.

Also it states that "the treatment is now also under test by Dr. Paul Magnuson at Chicago's Northwestern University, at Columbia University in New York under Dr. Ralph Boots, and by Dr. R. H. Freyberg at the University of Michigan. . . ."

Dr. de Kruif did not ask either Dr. Freyberg's or my opinion regarding our results. Reports have already been published from Dr. Freyberg's clinic, as well as from our own, concerning Ertron. Dr. Freyberg is certainly unenthusiastic concerning its value. . . . He states: "Of the many newer forms of treatment for chronic arthritis, one of the most highly advertised is treatment with massive doses of Vitamin D. I know of no rationale for such therapy" and "Results of this entire study of Vitamin D therapy are certainly far from impressive of great value in this form of treatment.''

The low opinion in which Drs. Boots and Freyberg held the treatment so optimistically described by the *Digest* could not, of course, have been known to many of the country's three million arthritis sufferers, hundreds of whom, according to an editorial in the A.M.A. *Journal,* promptly went to their physicians begging for the new treatment. ''Those who attempt education of the public in matters of health and disease,'' said the *Journal,* in this connection, ''have a serious responsibility; they do incalculable harm when they mislead the public.''

A few years ago, in furtherance of its campaign against syphilis, the *Digest,* whose early articles about this disease were praised by the A.M.A. as ''models for this type of discussion,'' published an article called ''Found: A One-Day Cure for Syphilis.'' This piece, described by the *Digest* as the ''medical sensation of the year,'' told of the apparently remarkable results of a new ten-hour treatment for syphilis, and added that ''Drs. Walter M. Simpson, H. Worley Kendell, and Donald

L. Rose of the Miami Valley Hospital are now reporting scientifically upon this epochal one-day treatment of syphilis.'' Actually, Drs. Simpson, Kendell, and Rose had already reported on the treatment. In an article published in the *British Journal of Venereal Diseases* twenty months before, they had said:

> At the present time such treatment should be considered strictly experimental.
>
> The results achieved thus far should stimulate other investigators to engage in long-term, controlled experiments with a view to the introduction of a more rapid, more certain, less dangerous and costly method of treatment.

In general, the medical profession greeted the *Digest's* medical sensation of the year with restraint. In an article published in the *Archives of Internal Medicine,* three syphilis specialists, in collaboration, said:

> With his usual uncritical judgment, hyper-enthusiasm and willingness prematurely to capitalize journalistically on sober scientific

experimentation, de Kruif has unhappily drawn nationwide attention to this "one-day cure" for syphilis. This tendency of medical journalists to raise false hopes in lay minds can only be deplored. With all due respect to democratic freedom of speech, it is too bad that no censorship exists to compel conservative accuracy from medical sensationalists.

Despite this unsympathetic professional attitude toward its medical articles, the *Digest* in 1944 worked up a certain amount of enthusiasm over a new treatment for tuberculosis, which it announced in a piece called "Diasone: New Hope for White Plague Victims." "*The most promising compound in the history of tuberculosis, yes,*" the article proclaimed, though it added, somewhat less emphatically and not in italics, that the drug "may develop dangerous side reactions or prove far less potent than present experience indicates." There was also a depressing addendum explaining that the drug would not be available to physicians in private practice for a year, but, since many people read as they run, physicians everywhere were immediately beset with pleas for the new drug and the headquarters of the National Tuberculosis Association in New York was overrun by patients and relatives of patients determined to get hold of the most promising compound in the history of tuberculosis. The medical section of the Association, the American Trudeau Society, which is made up of two thousand tuberculosis specialists, did not share the *Digest's* enthusiasm for the new drug. At a meeting held soon after the article appeared, Dr. H. Corwin Hinshaw, chairman of the Society's Committee on Therapy, presented a report which, he said, was made necessary by the unwarranted optimism of tuberculosis patients and their families about diasone as a cure for tuberculosis. "This degree of optimism is not expressed by those physicians who have used this drug clinically," Dr. Hinshaw began in his polite but firm and extended rebuke.

If physicians look upon *Digest* articles expounding the wonders of drugs that are not available and treatments that have not been tested as a mischievous medical strip tease, they take an even dimmer view of the magazine's suggestions for self-medication. The *Digest* attained what is probably its outstanding contribution to the art of self-medication in its May, 1942, issue, in an article called "A Working Cure for Athlete's Foot." This piece said that anyone could go to a drug-store and get the druggist to mix a fifty-fifty solu-tion of phenol and camphor which would be effica-cious in treating athlete's foot. A great many readers evidently began rushing to their druggists and daubing themselves with the recommended solution. The results were often astonishing. One woman who applied the *Digest's* solution one night found her feet swollen and painful the next, was admitted to a hospital a week later, remained there for thirteen days, and was, altogether, disabled for twenty-seven days. For this *Digest* fan, as well as for many others, the piece on athlete's foot will unquestionably remain an article of lasting interest.

The art of living, as *The Reader's Digest* has defined it, is the art of learning to live an upright life on next to nothing a year. In the *Digest* credo, spiritual poverty is boldly condemned. Though material poverty is not flatly endorsed, a rather strong case is made out for it. "I look back to my adventures in life," one piece in the art-of-living category goes, "and think of the happiest people I have met. They were mostly poverty-stricken." A longing for the happiness that comes from destitution has affected other *Digest* philosophers. "As I get older," one of them has said, "I sometimes wish something would reduce me to comparative poverty so I could flee the laminated multiplicities of my life as I have developed it." He added that if he couldn't be poverty-stricken, he wished at least that his house would burn down. What many people don't realize about poverty, the *Digest* has often pointed out, is that it is really good fun. The best things in life are free, and you can get so much pleasure from the little things. You can write letters, for instance: "One of the best things in life costs just three cents—sometimes only two. Plus the gracious impulse to write a letter, an unlooked-for letter, the kind of letter that brings to the lucky recipient a lift for the whole day." Or you can listen to children and become aware of yourself: "A four-year-old once asked me, 'Don't sleeves get tired of arms sometimes?' Funny—but significant, too. Become aware of yourself, of the way you button your coat, of how your feet feel inside of your shoes. When the breakfast eggs are frying, listen to them." Or you can take up a nature hobby and learn bird songs, raise ants, or collect shells and plants. Or, and perhaps most important, you can embark on a program of making friends: "No adventure in life is more interesting than meeting a new person. And that doesn't mean being presented to some glamorous movie idol. Talking with any plain Bob Harris of South Falls can be just as exciting—if you know how to get the kick out of it." The author of this last observation plainly knows how to get the kick out of it, for he tells how he met a Bob Harris type on a train and how, as this Harris happened to be in the insulation line, the two of them had a fascinating time discussing rock wool. Because material possessions are stumbling blocks on the road to the good, penurious life, people should get rid of them. If you own a car, dispose of it. "Having a car constantly at your disposal is like owning a pair of automatic crutches," and if you throw them away, the chances are that you will "discover the unexpected satisfactions of life *without* them." Of all the statements the *Digest* has printed on the art of living, none is more illuminating than one made by A. J. Cronin, the best-selling author, just before he disposed of the movie rights to another of his novels for two hundred thousand dollars. Mr. Cronin:

> We must have an ideology not based on superficial things, on printed paper money or overstuffed upholstery or underslung sedans, but on something deeper, vital, spiritual. Times are changing; values are in the melting pot. Amid the desolation of this war-torn world, let us remember that God fulfills himself in many ways. Christ cast the money-changers from the temple. We must cast out all self-interest from our lives. Today a man's best assets are his health, a stout heart, confidence in his own integrity. His only true capital is, was, and always will be his soul.

In this one brief paragraph, Mr. Cronin has captured the essence of the *Digest's* philosophy of life, a tidy compound of two ageless aphorisms: "Money isn't everything" and "What does it matter so long as you've got your health?"

The *Digest's* philosophy underwent its severest pragmatic test during the depression years, when many readers had a chance to experiment with a design for living on little or nothing a year. *Digest* articles of this period seem to prove that the philosophy of strength through poverty was handsomely vindicated. A Minneapolis pastor, for example, explained that a depression is a cause for gratitude:

> When the depression came I was compelled to take an invoice and soon discovered that I was still rich. All my capacity for the enjoyment of life was still intact. My $200,000 eyes are just as good as they ever were. . . . A $10,000 sense of hearing is still unimpaired. . . . Then there's my $1,000,000 stomach and a half-million-dollar appetite. . . .
>
> The last six months have been for many men a thrilling spiritual adventure through which they have discovered their real wealth. Bereft of dividends and profits, they are discovering the sustaining powers of a strong, religious faith, the abiding values of courage, heroism, charity, and trustworthiness.

The *Digest* printed many similar stories, among them one called "Not by Bread Alone," written by a young couple bereft of folding money, who told

what a grand time they were having on an income
of forty dollars a month, and one called "We Live
in the Slums," a dissertation on the charms of
poor housing.

Even in good times, the *Digest* keeps plugging
its concept of the art of living with stories about
people who have overcome monstrous misfortune.
A *Digest* article by the Reverend Harry Emerson
Fosdick demonstrated what a sound practice this
is. He remarked:

> The most stimulating successes in history
> have come from persons who, facing some
> kind of limitations and handicaps, took them
> as part of life's game and played splendidly
> in spite of them. Once when Ole Bull, the
> great violinist, was giving a concert in Paris,
> his A-string snapped and he transposed the
> composition and finished it on three strings.
> That is life—to have your A-string snap and
> finish on three strings.

The majority of the characters in the *Digest's*
art-of-living series are poor, honest, earnest, and
spunky. They have A-string trouble, but play on

as splendidly as Bull. Next to the plucky, two-fisted clergymen who often take the leading roles in *Digest* stories, the most typical *Digest* heroes and heroines are probably those whose chronicles appear in the biographical department called "The Most Unforgettable Character I've Met." Among these enduring characters are Emmy, a gifted Eskimo able to catch trout with her bare hands, and a Samoan girl named Fialelei, a lovely creature who had a habit of "bravely laughing through the tears that rolled down her cheeks" and was such a decent sort that her presence "was like having Christ in the house." As a rule, however, *Digest* characters are not exotic. Kathleen Norris's most unforgettable character was her Aunt Batty, Albert Payson Terhune's was one of man's best friends named Sunnybank Bobby, and Channing Pollock's was an Englishman in Malaya who banked a thousand dollars a day and was, of course, miserable.

Edwin Balmer, the editor of *Redbook,* has had the good fortune to meet more than one most unforgettable character. In 1942, he wrote an article for the *Digest* in which he said the most unforgettable person he ever encountered was a woman named Winnie, his childhood nurse; the following year, he decided that his mother was more most unforgettable than his nurse, and sold another piece. In the opinion of many readers, the most unforgettable person the *Digest* ever reported on was a lady a *Digest* writer met on shipboard and wrote about for the magazine's "Drama in Real Life" department. This character was an armless woman who surprised some of her fellow-passengers by knitting, writing letters, powdering her nose, and playing bridge with her feet. After inquiring about the lady's interesting talents, the author said that he complimented her for demonstrating "the wonderful strength the human spirit has," and added, "Her eyes filled with tears at that, but she smiled as she raised her handkerchief in her right foot, wiped her eyes, and then blew her nose stridently. We both laughed."

Judging by what the *Digest* has printed, Wallace's own most unforgettable character is Henry Ford. Wallace has printed more articles about Ford than about any other man, woman, child, or beast—an average of about two a year. In the first issue of his little magazine, Wallace published "Henry Ford, Dreamer and Worker." Since then, he has kept his readers in close touch with his hero through articles such as "Ford Discusses Human Flivvers," "Henry Ford Talks to Young Men," "Ford Explores the Farm Riddle," "What Is Ford Doing Now?," "What Is Ford Going to Do?," "Why Doesn't Ford Quit?," "Are Gandhi and Ford on the Same Road?," and "Mr. Ford Doesn't Care." The *Digest's* articles on Ford have ranged from laudatory to very laudatory. The admiration, apparently, is mutual. Ford reads the *Digest* and has endorsed it. "I look forward to each issue of your little publication with much pleasure," he informed Wallace a few years ago in a letter, "and I find in your selection of articles two things: interpretations of the present and indications of the future."

The indications of the future of *The Reader's Digest* are clear from interpretations of the present: What Ford has done in automobile manufacturing, Wallace has done and is trying to do in publishing. Ford gave Everyman a car he could drive, Wallace gave Everyman some literature he could read; both turned the trick with mass production. Ford got to the top by standardizing engines, Wallace by standardizing ideas. Wallace has already made history by adapting the assembly-line technique to the production of literature, but he will make more, because he has that thing called know-how. In its development, *The Reader's Digest* of today is still in about the Model T stage. Like the Ford, the *Digest* will no doubt eventually become a slicker item. Instead of planting only some of its articles in other magazines in order to "reprint" them, it may plant them all, thus safeguarding the *Digest* against the intrusion of any thoughts or opinions that did not originate on the premises. This would be fine not only for the *Digest* but also for the other magazines, which would begin to look more and more as though they had caught on to the magic formula. Perhaps, as the little magazine continues to grow, there will appear, on the site of the *Digest's* present headquarters in Chappaqua, a great new plant, a River Rouge for the mass production of belles-lettres. There Wallace and his staff will manufacture ideas with interchangeable parts and ship them out to the world. People everywhere will think alike. And what happens where all think alike? The answer to that is simple, or at least simplistic. In the March, 1934, issue of *The Reader's Digest,* Walter Lippmann said: "Where all think alike, no one thinks very much."